1. A Way of Desert Spirituality

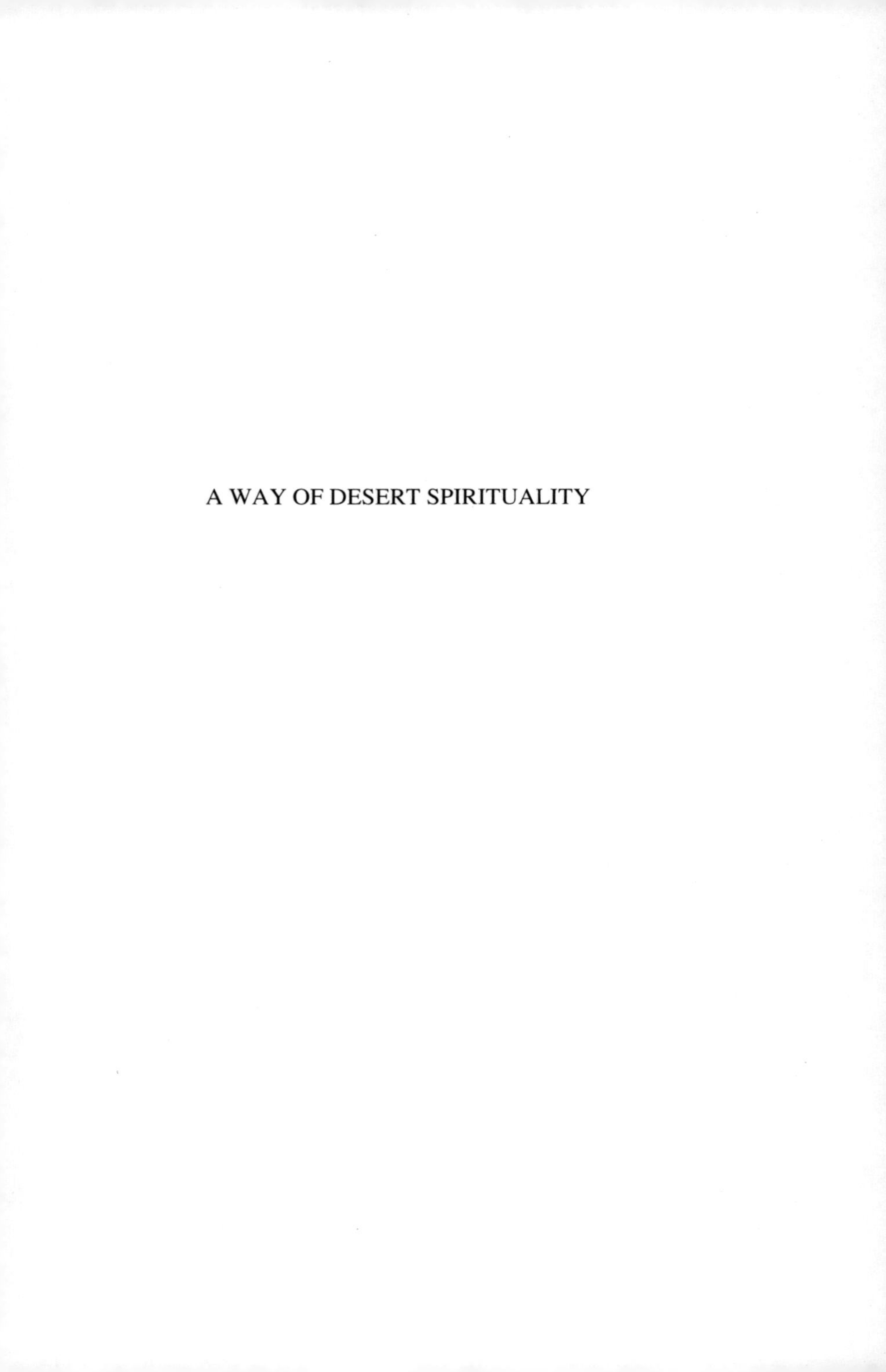

A WAY OF DESERT SPIRITUALITY

A Way of Desert Spirituality

THE RULE OF LIFE

of the Hermits of Bethlehem of the Heart of Jesus

ALBA · HOUSE NEW · YORK

SOCIETY OF ST. PAUL, 2187 VICTORY BLVD., STATEN ISLAND, NY 10314

Library of Congress Cataloging-in-Publication Data

Romano, Eugene L.
A way of desert spirituality : the rule of life of the Hermits of Bethlehem of the Heart of Jesus / Eugene L. Romano.
p. cm.
ISBN 0-8189-0661-8
1. Hermits of Bethlehem of the Heart of Jesus — Rules.
2. Monasticism and religious orders — Rules. I. Title.
BX3674.5.R65 1992
255'.79 — dc20 92-37733
CIP

Nihil Obstat:
Joan Kerwin Lawler, CSJP, JCL
Censor Librorum

Imprimatur:
† Most Rev. Frank J. Rodimer, DD, JCD
Bishop of Paterson, New Jersey
June 26, 1992

The Nihil Obstat and Imprimatur are official declarations that a book or pamphlet is free of doctrinal or moral error. No implication is contained therein that those who have granted the Nihil Obstat and Imprimatur agree with the contents, opinions or statements expressed.

Produced and designed in the United States of America by the Fathers and Brothers of the Society of St. Paul, 2187 Victory Boulevard, Staten Island, New York 10314, as part of their communications apostolate.

ISBN: 0-8189-0661-8

Printing Information:

Current Printing - first digit	2	3	4	5	6	7	8	9	10

Year of Current Printing - first year shown

1993 1994 1995 1996 1997

OFFICE OF THE BISHOP

PATERSON DIOCESAN CENTER
777 VALLEY ROAD
CLIFTON, NEW JERSEY 07013

Rev. Eugene Romano, H.B.H.J.
Bethlehem Hermitage
P. O. Box 314
Chester, New Jersey 07930

Dear Father Gene:

The Rule and Statutes of the Hermits of Bethlehem describe a way of life to which relatively few disciples of Jesus are called to follow strictly. However, it is a way of life that will appeal to a much greater number of his disciples who desire a closer union with God as He reveals Himself to them and calls them, as He has called men and women for centuries, to find Him and stay with Him in the desert.

The scope of the Rule is far greater than that of a legislative manual. It is the fruit of your lived experience over the course of many years, especially at Bethlehem in Chester. In that time you have delved into the Scriptures, studied the lives and writings of the prophets, probed the hearts and minds of the early desert fathers and mothers, united yourself to Jesus in the Eucharist and called upon Mary, his mother and ours, to help you absorb the spirit of the simple life that she, Joseph and Jesus lived in Bethlehem.

People need simplicity today more than ever before. The pace of life is frantic. The schedule most people keep is exhausting. The desires spurred by commerce are insatiable. This frenetic pace makes more and more people stop to ask, "Where is God? How can I find Him? How can I get some peace?" The message of God to the shepherds two millenia ago comes down to us today: "Go to Bethlehem!"

Many shepherds of souls and wise men and women, as well, will make their way to Bethlehem in Chester, but even if they don't or can't, they now have in this published Rule a way to discover God and the love His Spirit gives. For this I hope and pray as I give my approval to the Bethlehem Rule and Statutes.

Fraternally in Christ,

+ Frank J. Rodimer

Most Rev. Frank J. Rodimer
Bishop of Paterson

June 26, 1992
Solemnity of the Sacred Heart of Jesus

To the Glory
of the
Triune God
Father, Son, and Holy Spirit
with praise
to the Virgin Mary,
Mother of the Divine Child of Bethlehem
and
Joseph,
father of the Holy Family.

FOREWORD

A resurgence of interest in the eremitical life within the Church has occurred as God stirs the hearts of many individuals to make a radical choice to live the Gospel. Bethlehem is a return to the same desert that called to the Christians of the third and fourth centuries. Unlike the many programs, activities and weekend experiences that define so much of spirituality in our age, Bethlehem stands as a doorway to the wilderness of your own heart. It is an anointed place where you can empty your mind, heart and soul into the infinitely loving presence of the Triune God.

In our day, Holy Mother the Church has recognized the hermit lifestyle as an action of the Holy Spirit and has given her blessing to this way of life. It is the first time in the history of the Church that hermits have been codified by Canon Law (Canon 603). Pope Paul VI, of saintly memory, and Pope John Paul II have both encouraged and supported this very special ministry of prayer in the silence and solitude of the eremitical life. One of the fruits of this are the many lauras (colonies) of hermits springing up worldwide like desert flowers.

Clergy, religious and laity of every walk of life enter the desert of Bethlehem and ask: *How can I bring this way of life home with me to be integrated with my own busy life?* After years of living the eremitical way of Bethlehem day to day, we have distilled our experience into this book: *A Way of Desert Spirituality.*

We are convinced that, just as the Bethlehem Hermitage is a grace conferred on us, the Hermits of Bethlehem of the Heart of Jesus, to share with the world, so, too, is our *Rule of Life*. More, we perceive that many are searching for what we have been granted.

The Spirit of God present in Bethlehem quiets the mind, opens the heart and heals the soul. *A Way of Desert Spirituality* is a loving response to this action. We believe that, because it is of God, it is unique. In a world of delectable distractions that promise much while poisoning the soul, here is a *Rule of Life* with the power to heal, not by pleasing or entertaining appearance, but with the dry but nourishing bread of the desert.

The reader is therefore challenged to discard contemporary perspectives and to enter the true desert of the heart where the living water of the Word of God is the only water, and familiar landmarks dissolve in the intensity of God's own silence and solitude.

TABLE OF CONTENTS

Rule of Life of the Hermits of Bethlehem of the Heart of Jesus

Statutes

PREFACE

During my retreat of Holy Week in 1975 at the Trappist Monastery in Spencer, Massachusetts, I was already set on my course to begin an eremitical foundation named "Bethlehem" on eighteen and a half acres of land in Chester, New Jersey, and I had come to Spencer to prepare myself spiritually for the work God was calling me to do. On Good Friday of that week I was present for Vigils at 3:00 a.m. in the monastery church when the reader came to a passage from St. Jerome's *Treatise on Psalm 95* that stirred me deeply. "Blessed is the one who bears the Cross and Resurrection in one's heart, as well as the place of the Birth and Ascension of Christ. Blessed is the one who possesses Bethlehem in one's heart and in whose heart Christ is born daily. For what is the meaning of Bethlehem if not 'House of Bread'? Let us, too, be a house of bread, of that Bread which came down from heaven."

When I first heard those words, I felt they were a wonderful confirmation of my hope and my calling from God. Now, seventeen years later, they have been even more wonderfully confirmed by the foundation of the Hermits of Bethlehem of the Heart of Jesus whose Rule of Life is published in this book. This Rule was written for hermits — men and women who have been led into the desert to follow God in silence and solitude. Not only is the Rule a juridical document, but more importantly, it is an attempt to unfold the charism of the desert in the framework of a lived experience, theirs and mine. The Rule is a spiritual reflection of our way of life.

It is always difficult to find the right words to express the way God is leading His people. Never before in my life have I been more conscious of the Spirit groaning within me as I did when writing this document. While it emerged from lived experience as the fruit of contemplation, I am keenly aware of my own unworthiness and sinfulness. At the same time I am overwhelmed by the sense of the Holy Spirit's presence. In my heart I know and believe the Holy Spirit has been working through me to glorify God. Indeed, to accomplish His will, "God chose those whom the world considers weak and foolish to confound the strong and wise" (1 Corinthians 1:27).

Bethlehem is a humble place. The prophet Micah wrote that Bethlehem-ephrathah was "too small among the clans of Judah" to become the birthplace of the "one who is to be ruler of Israel" (Micah 5:1). Yet Micah's absurd prophecy became a reality. Bethlehem Hermitage must have seemed similarly absurd as it first took shape as a dream, as a hope and then as a tentative plan.

As a young seminarian and later as a parish priest I felt a persistent desire for the contemplative life. The desire for prayerful solitude and the quiet adoration of the hidden Lord in the Holy Eucharist seemed to conflict with my vocation to the diocesan priesthood. In 1967, ten years after my ordination, I spent a vacation period with the Trappists in Spencer to see whether or not I had a monastic vocation. It was a beautiful community, and I felt strongly attracted to this classical form of contemplative religious life, yet I felt the Lord was leading me in a different direction.

In 1968 I approached Bishop Lawrence B. Casey of Paterson with an idea of a diocesan hermitage. He was sympathetic but was short of priests and asked me to set the idea aside while accepting a pastoral assignment. In 1973 the matter was raised again, and this time Bishop Casey agreed. He wrote to the people in my parish saying: "There is no doubt that Father's decision came after many years of prayerful consideration, and I am convinced that his is a special call from God which will bring many future blessings to our diocese...."

Six months after formal approval was given by the bishop a generous donor expressed the wish to give the diocese a large parcel of beautiful woodland in Chester, New Jersey. The following March, I moved into a farmhouse on the property, and a few short weeks later God's blessing on Bethlehem seemed confirmed by St. Jerome's words on Good Friday in Spencer.

The physical work of creating Bethlehem Hermitage as a place where people could stay and find prayerful solitude took several years. A road was constructed, then four hermitages, then a common house and four more hermitages. The chapel of Our Lady of Bethlehem was dedicated by Bishop Frank Rodimer of Paterson on June 5, 1981 who had succeeded Bishop Casey. By 1984 there were twelve hermitages, with more buildings in the planning stages.

Over the years hundreds of people had come to live and pray at Bethlehem, some for short periods and some for long stretches of time. The original mustard seed of solitude and contemplation had grown through different stages and was now blossoming into an eremitical laura of hermits. This style of religious life is not monastic, strictly speaking, but hearkens back to the ancient tradition of desert fathers and mothers of North Africa in the fourth century and of Palestine centuries before.

Bishop Rodimer approved the Statutes of the Hermits of Bethlehem of the Heart of Jesus in October of 1989. As this is written, Bethlehem is home to three hermits in perpetual public vows, living on a daily basis the Rule you hold in your hands. Other men and women are in different stages of discernment regarding a vocation to the Bethlehem Hermit way of life.

I invite you — hermits and non-hermits alike — to reflect on this Rule in such a way that it becomes a lived experience for you. May it become life-giving for you and bring you closer to God.

A hermit's life is special. Just as Jesus is the perfect gift of the Father's love, so do we who feel drawn to the eremitical life desire to imitate Jesus by giving ourselves to God completely. It is the burning desire of the Heart of Jesus to reveal and to communicate God's love for us, bringing us together into the intimate family of the Triune God. As Hermits of Bethlehem of the Heart of Jesus we are invited to "gift ourselves" back to God. Jesus exemplifies extravagant selflessness. We seek to love as He loves.

Through the hidden life of prayer in the silence of solitude, we hermits strive for purity of heart that mirrors the Heart of Jesus. We do this in the daily offering and surrendering of our lives to God. Although solitaries, we are consecrated "for the salvation of the world" where people are isolated from each other and from God by hatred and sin. Solitaries are not isolated people. We are whole people, united with God and with suffering humanity. Our prayer echoes Christ's prayer "that all may be one in us, that the world may believe you sent me" (John 17:21). In the midst of a troubled world we hermits desire to give witness by our lives of prayer and solitude to the absoluteness of God. God alone can satisfy the longings of truth and love. The hermit life is one that depends on God alone to be faithful to His commandments. In this way we please our Heavenly Father and are safeguarded against attacks from within or without.

The hermit vocation really does not need justification. Neither does the Laura of Hermits of Bethlehem. We are simply men and women who have heard within ourselves the unmistakable call from God and who have responded in love. Since it is God alone who asks, and simply because God has asked, that is reason enough.

Our life of solitude and separation from the world, of unceasing prayer and penance in union with Jesus, is the power that brings about the conversion and transformation of the Body of Christ, the Church. We hermits are invited to enter the desert of our hearts in order to build up the Church and to fulfill our lives.

May Mary, the Mother of the Incarnate Word and our own mother, be our exemplar as we strive to be disciples of her loving Son, Jesus.

Rev. Eugene C.L. Romano, HBHJ
Desert Father of Bethlehem

PROLOGUE

The Hermits of Bethlehem of the Heart of Jesus

A way of life based on the Gospel of Jesus Christ and lived in the tradition and spirit of the Desert Fathers and Mothers of the early Church.

The hermit is one called by God in imitation of Jesus to live a life of unceasing prayer and penance in the silence of solitude for the praise of God and the salvation of the world. It is a life lived in greater separation from the world in the Heart of God and in the heart of the Church for the Church.

The hermit life emerged during the 4th and 5th centuries in Egypt, Asia Minor, Syria and Palestine. Previously, thousands of Christians were martyred as they shed their blood for the sake of Christ and His Kingdom. To a world of persecuted Christians, the Emperor Constantine brought peace and cessation of bloodshed for the faith.

When the persecution ceased, the Church still had to face the great danger that confronts her even to this day, namely, to live in the world without compromise. **"The world continued to prefer the darkness to the light"** (John 3:19). Because of this threat to the authentic following of Christ and His holy Gospel, many fled into the solitude of the deserts, and thus a school of desert spirituality was forged.

These men and women strove to imitate the lives of the great prophets: Elijah, St. John the Baptist, and above all Jesus Christ Himself. Like the Exodus of Israel led by Moses in the Desert of Sinai, where they wandered for forty years, they saw their own exodus in following Jesus, their Model, Who was **"led by the Spirit to be tempted"** (Matthew 4:1).

It was their burning desire for God that led the solitaries into the deserts of Judea, Syria and Egypt and these deserts became the dwelling place for thousands of solitaries.

Since the world as persecutor was no longer the enemy of the Christian, the Christian had to become the enemy of the dark world. In the desert the Christian became a new kind of martyr giving witness to the saving power of the Risen Christ against the destructive powers of evil.

The school of desert spirituality which was emerging became the foundation of the eremitical and monastic life which took different forms. The Laura, which was a colony of hermits under obedience to a desert father, was one of the emerging forms of life.

ST. ANTHONY THE GREAT

Among the great Fathers of the Desert was St. Anthony the Great. He is one of the patrons and examples of the Hermits of Bethlehem. What we know of St. Anthony is from the classic biography written by St. Athanasius, Bishop of Alexandria.

St. Athanasius wrote that "You also, once you have heard the story, will not merely admire the man, but will wish to emulate his resolution as well." Athanasius presents in his biography a model of life consecrated to God. St. Anthony's life was written as a model for monastic and solitary living. St. Augustine, in his *Confessions*, tells us that the book had a definite influence on his own conversion and on the vocations of others who were seeking God.

St. Anthony was born around the year 250 in Comus, Upper Egypt. At the age of twenty St. Anthony was so moved by the Gospel message read in Church, **"Go, sell what you have and give it to the poor"** (Matthew 19:21), that he immediately responded to God's word and distributed his rich inheritance — and he also provided for his sister by placing her with a group of consecrated virgins.

Anthony lived in solitude some distance from his village and there spent his time in reading the Scriptures, prayer and penance. He engaged in manual labor in order to earn his food. He sought the advice and example of other outstanding hermits and strove in competition to imitate their virtues of prayer, fasting, mortification, silence, etc.

Though Anthony preferred solitude, he was much sought after for spiritual guidance and healing. Disciples built their hermitages in the vicinity of Anthony's. St. Anthony formed them into a (Laura), a group of solitaries, and led them in the way of perfection and holiness.

When asked for guidance, St. Anthony related stories to depict a point of centrality in living out the Christian vocation. Because his wisdom was rooted in the Scriptures, his teachings give witness to the truth of God's revelation. The sayings were later written down and shared with others. The wisdom of such sayings is still relevant as it communicates the essence of living in and for God.

St. Anthony assisted St. Athanasius in combatting the Arian Heresy. He had a great desire to be a martyr and in the Roman persecution of 311, he exposed himself to great danger while giving spiritual and material support to those in prison. Though Anthony's desire to be a martyr was never fulfilled, he "went back to his solitary cell and there he was a daily martyr to his conscience, ever fighting the battles of faith."

At the age of 60 Anthony withdrew farther into the Egyptian desert and lived in greater solitude where he practiced a zealous and more intense and ascetical life. He dwelt in the tombs where he suffered many temptations against all sorts of demons. Like Jesus, he was **"led into the desert by the Spirit to be tempted by the devil"** (Matthew 4:1).

After many years in seeking God through prayer, penance and combatting the demons, he emerged out of the desert a healthy man in body, mind and spirit. St. Athanasius writes: "Strangers knew him from among his disciples by the joy on his face." He renounced the world to serve God in the solitude of the desert and was called "the friend of God." In 356 he died in solitude at the age of 105.

We pray "Father, you called St. Anthony to renounce the world and serve you in the solitude of the desert. By his prayers and example may we learn to deny ourselves and to love you above all things." (Opening Prayer of the Mass)

"Lord, you helped St. Anthony conquer the powers of darkness. Strengthen us in our struggle with evil." (Communion Prayer of the Mass)

Desert Spirituality

Today, in our times we are experiencing a new phenomenon in the Church throughout the world; that is, a return to the desert.

Among the reasons for flight into the desert were:

- to prepare and hasten the Parousia, the Coming of the Lord; to encounter the Risen Christ
- to be living martyrs giving a radical witness to the Gospel; to live out faithfully the teachings of Christ in simplicity and poverty of heart. "The martyrdom of the heart is no less fruitful than the martyrdom of blood" - St. Therese.
- to maintain the integrity of the Christian life; to give witness to the Absoluteness of God
- to strengthen the Church which was becoming mediocre due to assimilation of worldly ways, ideologies and state recognition
- to live a life of prayer for their own personal sanctification and for the Church; to embrace the concerns of the Heart of Christ, making His prayer their own: **"...that they may be one, as we are one..."** (John 17:22).
- to live a penitential life for one's own sake and the Church by responding with love to His Word in the way of the ascetics: **"Renounce yourself, take up your cross and follow me"** (Matthew 16:24).

"...to fill up what is lacking in the sufferings of Christ" (Colossians 1:24).

- to seek God alone **"O God, You are my God whom I seek"** (Psalm 63:2) and to be faithful to His commandments, thereby safeguarding oneself against the attacks of the demons from within and without. **"Therefore, submit to God; resist the devil and he will take flight"** (James 4:7). **"Your opponent the devil is prowling about like a roaring lion looking for someone to devour"** (1 Peter 5:8).

The spirituality of the desert is not based on a system of practices or doctrine that could be learned and applied to daily living. The spirituality of the desert was caught, not taught. It was a whole way of life and was the hard work of a lifetime of lived experience in and of the Lord. It was a holistic approach to spirituality of striving to direct every aspect of body, mind and soul to God.

The desert fathers* accepted the challenge of the Gospel with generosity and singleness of purpose and responded to it with their entire being without compromise. They strove to be obedient to the Word and the spirit of the Gospel with their entire lives.

The integration of the whole person toward God was effected by continual prayer. Abba Agathon said, "Prayer is hard and a great struggle to one's last breath."

---

* Whenever the masculine is used, the feminine can be substituted, e.g., Desert Father/Mother; Spiritual Father/Mother; hermit/hermitess.

The Laura

The Laura is a colony of hermits living in separate solitary dwellings (hermitages) surrounding a central chapel and common house, united in the love of the Heart of Christ and under obedience to the Desert Father.

Why a Laura?

- The hermits provide encouragement for one another in living a solitary vocation of prayer and penance for the Church.
- They gather for and are strengthened by Word and Eucharist Sacrifice.
- The Laura provides opportunities to exercise loving charity and hospitality. [The ancient hermits were about what any Christian at any time in history must be about - love of God and neighbor.]
- The hermits offer practical support for each other: e.g., the aged and sick.
- They are protected from intruders (marauders, thieves, curiosity seekers, hunters, satanic cults, drug addicts, etc.)

Desert Teachings and Writings

As hermits whose lives are based on the Gospel of Jesus Christ and lived in the tradition and spirit of the desert fathers of the early Church, we pay special attention to their writings and teachings.

These early Christians desired to focus their lives on the love of God which drew them to Himself. Through this love, they were empowered to love God and others and so share with others the great depths of God's love. By living their lives through, with and in Him, they reflected His radiance to others.

The desert writings and teachings are based on stories about the desert fathers and their sayings. These writings were originally meant for specific individuals who came to the desert seeking guidance. The sayings were later written down and shared with others.

Often the desert fathers related stories to depict a point of centrality in living out the Christian vocation. Because the fathers were rooted in Scripture, their teachings give witness to the truth of God's revelation. The wisdom of such sayings is still relevant as it communicates the essence of living in and for God.

Withdrawing from the world to seek God more intimately, these early desert fathers drew on the rich blessings of their relationship with God. The fruits of their contemplation were shared with those who came seeking spiritual or secular advice on how to **"live in the world but not of the world"** (John 17:11,14).

As contemporary hermits, we too have withdrawn from the world to seek God more intimately. Drawing strength and wisdom from Scripture and the desert writings and teachings in prayerful silence and solitude, we hope to share with others, through our desert hospitality, the depth and beauty of communion with God.

The Eremitical Way of Life of the Hermits of Bethlehem

The Hermits of Bethlehem live their eremitical way of life according to the new Code of Canon Law - 603, which deals specifically with hermits. This canon can address either one hermit or a Laura, that is, a colony of hermits. The bishop of a diocese receives the consecration of a hermit with the hermit's plan of life.

Bishop Frank J. Rodimer has approved the plan of life of the Hermits of Bethlehem and has received the perpetual public vows of the hermits, according to our Statutes and Rule of Life. The bishop has also stated that the Hermits of Bethlehem represent a new charism in the Church.

We see our way of life as primarily eremitical, solitary. The only times the hermits come together is for daily Mass preceded by Lauds (Morning Prayer), Solemn Vespers on Thursday nights and for a common meal on Sundays in the spirit of the Desert Fathers. All other times of prayer, work and meals are accomplished in total solitude. Each hermit lives, prays and works alone to maintain the solitary spirit.

Each hermit is under the direction of the Desert Father and is guided according to one's own needs. The Desert Father, with the hermit, under the guidance of the Holy Spirit, discern how to live one's particular life within the Laura by a plan; i.e., the Rule and charism of Bethlehem.

While there is a Rule and Horarium, the hermit life is lived out by each hermit in an individual, solitary way within the Laura, thereby supporting one another in solitude. The hermit strives to accomplish this with a level of mature, responsible freedom to adapt the Rule and the Horarium in order to maximize one's living out of the charism of the Hermits of Bethlehem. This flexibility is distinct from cenobitical monastic living, wherein all exercises are experienced in common and in regularity.

In the hermit's life of solitude we are always striving to seek God above all for His own sake. We strive to live every moment in His holy presence, seeking purity of heart, in order to grow in the perfection of charity.

INTRODUCTION

When Jesus was asked by one of the scribes, **"Which is the first of all the commandments?" Jesus replied, "This is the first: 'Hear, O Israel! The Lord our God is Lord alone! Therefore, you shall love the Lord your God with all your heart, with all your soul, with all your mind, and with all your strength.' This is the second, 'You shall love your neighbor as yourself.' There is no commandment greater than these."** (Mark 12:28-31).

The answer Jesus gave is based on Deuteronomy 6:4-5, and is known as the SHEMA ISRAEL. For the Jewish people, the key word in the commandment of love is SHEMA. 'Hear' — 'Listen' — 'Be Present To.'

The hermit's life is lived in a trinity of presence:

- Presence to God as our all-loving Creator and Father (to live a contemplative way of life)
- Presence to God in oneself as beloved of the Father (integrated wholeness of body, mind and spirit)
- Presence to God in others as the people of God (charity and hospitality)

This presence to God's grace elicits the response to become disciples in living His commandment of Love:

- Love of God above all for His own sake
- Love of oneself as a child of God
- Love of others as Jesus loves us

Our heavenly Father commands us, **"This is my Son, My Chosen One. Listen to Him"** (Luke 9:35). By listening to the Heart of Jesus, the hermits enter into the ongoing process of learning that they are loved and forgiven, welcomed back and recreated in His love. **"Learn from Me, for I am gentle and humble of heart... your souls will find rest"** (Matthew 11:29).

Listening is an expression of our loving openness to God, to ourselves, and to others. In each instance, the focus is on God. He becomes the center of our attention, the center from which all our actions flow. Nourished by Jesus, the bread of Life, the Hermit of Bethlehem is able to make the commandment of love the norm for daily living.

"As the Father has loved me, so I have loved you. Live on in my love" (John 15:9).

It was LOVE who gave us Jesus to be born in the Manger of Bethlehem. It was LOVE who died for us on the Cross and rose again from the dead, and it is in this LOVE the Hermit of Bethlehem desires to live.

CHAPTER I

The Hermit of Bethlehem will strive to be a living Bethlehem Presence to God as our all loving Creator and Father

(To Live a Contemplative Way of Life)

God in His great love, invites us to be present (listen) to Him with all the power of our being — mind, heart, spirit and strength.

> **"All you who are thirsty, come to the Water! ...Heed me and you shall eat well; you shall delight in rich fare. Come to Me heedfully, Listen, that you may have life."** (Isaiah 55:1-3)

It is very clear that God is telling us if we really wish to be nourished and enter into life with Him, we must be a people with *listening, loving hearts.*

This goal of presence (listening) to God is attained by freely allowing our spirits to be nourished on the following:

A. The Bread of Creation
B. The Bread of the "Desert Wilderness Experience" Found in the Silence and Solitude of the Hermitage
C. The Bread of Prayer and Contemplation Found in Communion with God Throughout the Day and Night

- Bread of the Word and Bread of the Eucharist
- Liturgy of the Hours
- Sacrament of Reconciliation

D. Our Lady of Bethlehem: Mother of the Incarnate Word and Our Mother

A. THE BREAD OF CREATION

God in His infinite love and wisdom created the universe. We are made to His image and likeness (Genesis 1:26). He loved us into being and sustains us in the midst of His world.

> **"God looked at everything that He had made and found it very pleasing."** (Genesis 1:31)

The energy of God pulsates in all of the animate nature of plants, trees, animals, birds, crying out to those who listen, **"...in Him we live and move and have our being."** (Acts 17:28)

God speaks to us through His marvelous creation, the things He has made, the world of nature.

> **"All the works of His hands speak of Him."**
> (Psalm 19)

Let creation be for us a book of learning about God. Jesus Himself gave His teaching by using many examples from the created things around Him: the flowers of the fields, the birds of the air, the animals, the seed, wheat, mountains, the sea and the fish, the vine and the branches. As bread nurtures our bodies so creation nurtures, heals and quiets our spirits, lifting them up in prayer to our Creator. It is only a listening spirit, a loving awareness, that will enable us to be inspired by the many voices of God's creation. Immersed in the silence of God's creation we can empty our heart into the Heart of God and experience His healing presence.

Creation is not just an event of long ago; creation is happening now at every moment. Listen to the work of His Hands in all of creation. Take notice of the birds, smell the flowers, walk in the woods, smell the pine, listen to the brook, take a leaf, touch a rock, watch the sunset, look up at the stars, feel the rain drops and snow flakes, listen to the rhythm of your body, your heartbeat. They speak of God leading us into silent adoration of the all-wise and Holy Creator.

> **"Let all creation bless the Lord, praise Him and magnify Him forever."** (*Benedicite*, Daniel 3:57)

B. THE BREAD OF THE "DESERT WILDERNESS" FOUND IN THE SILENCE AND SOLITUDE OF THE HERMITAGE

> **"I will espouse you (in faith), lead you into the desert and there I will speak to your heart."**
> (Hosea 2:14)

Just as creation is a means for opening to God and leading to silent adoration, so too the "Hermitage" is a sacred place that engenders an atmosphere of silence and desert-like solitude where one may **"Be still and know that the Lord is near."** (Psalm 46:10)

In the biblical sense, "desert wilderness" is a term

used to designate a place of solitude. The words desert, forest, woodlands, mountains are used symbolically to signify a solitary place. God leads a person into solitude when He wishes to enter into close relationship with him.

> **"I will give you hidden treasures and the concealed riches of secret places."** (Isaiah 45:3)

Solitude is the crucible of purification, preparing the hermit to see the Face of God. There is a difference between being alone for God and just being alone. Aloneness is for one great purpose: to develop a heart just for God.

SOLITUDE OF THE HERMITAGE

The Hermits of Bethlehem live as a Laura, that is, hermits living in separate, solitary dwellings around a central chapel, united in the love of the Heart of Jesus, the Incarnate Word.

The hermitage is a solitary dwelling place of the Spirit, that sacred place where the hermit seeks God, but more important, allows oneself to be found by Him.

In imitation of Jesus who **"...often retired to deserted places and prayed"** (Luke 5:16), the Hermit of Bethlehem desires to follow Jesus into His solitude and prayer in the presence of the Father. Jesus invites us **"to pray to our Father in secret."** (Matthew 6:5) The "hermitage" is the concrete expression of the hermit's desire and the place where solitude and prayer with Jesus becomes a reality. The "hermitage" is the wellspring of the Hermit's way of life. We must make the hermitage our dwelling place, our home, where the Lord will speak to our hearts.

> **"More than all else, keep watch over your heart, since here are the well-springs of life."**
>
> (Proverbs 4:23)

The hermitage/cell is the solitary's meeting place with God, where the hermit will come to know and love Him in the depths and silence of one's heart. The hermit will live in a deeper awareness, the truth of Jesus' words: **"Anyone who loves me will be true to my word, and my Father will love him; we will come to him and make our dwelling place with him."** (John 14:23)

The Divine Indwelling of the Trinity in the soul is the reason for the solitude of the hermitage. The Holy Spirit is our Divine Teacher, Who quietly guides and sanctifies us. The soul is the true temple of the Trinity where adoration of God in spirit and truth is nurtured. The hermit will strive under the guidance of the Holy Spirit to nurture this contemplative, solitary way, keeping alive that interior conversation with God, which gives meaning to the eremitical life.

It is when they are nourished by Word, Eucharist, prayer, work, fraternal joy, the hermits are gradually led more deeply into the mystery of God's love. In this solitude of the hermitage/cell, the hermit is alone with God and is formed by His loving action within the hermit's deepest self.

Unless the hermit has responsibility outside of one's hermitage, (those who may be engaged in the daily work of the Laura, such as receiving guests), the hermit remains in the hermitage occupied with prayer, lectio study or work.

> "*Sit in your cell and it will teach you everything.*"
> (Abba Moses)

The hermitage is not a place to do as one pleases, but to lose ourselves in God and make ourselves available to Him. Our time as hermits is never our own, doing what we want, or as we please, which is the spirit of the world, but always to do His Will.

The hermit's life is one of simplicity. With singleness of purpose, the hermit's complete orientation in the hermitage, (whether we pray, work, eat, sleep, etc.) is directed towards God, seeking Him in all things so our whole life becomes a praise of His glory.

The Hermits of Bethlehem enter solitude with an intense yearning for God. The hermit is not in isolation, but in communion with the Body of Christ, with the serious responsibility to pray for the Church. We humbly make intercession in the presence of the Father for His mercy and blessing upon ourselves and everyone whom Christ has redeemed by His death and resurrection.

GREATER SOLITUDE

Within the Laura of hermits, guided by the Holy Spirit, and under the discretion and direction of the Desert Father a perpetually professed hermit who has lived and been tested for a long period of time within the Laura and who has an ardent zeal for prayer, penance and seeking a stricter way to attain the perfection of charity may enter into greater solitude.

The hermit who has the grace of God to withdraw into reclusion will be freed from all cares and responsibilities within the Laura. The Desert Father will provide for all the necessities of the hermit, both material and spiritual. The hermit will live in strict obedience to the Desert Father so as not to follow one's own judgment, ideas, or desires without the express permission of the Desert Father. The reclusion can be for a temporary period of time or permanent.

Retreat

Annually for two periods of eight days, the professed hermits will enter into retreat. These retreats free the hermit from all work responsibilities.

Separation from the World

Abiding by the Code 603 the hermits withdraw into greater separation from the world to devote their lives to assiduous prayer and penance in the silence of solitude to the praise of God and the salvation of the world.

Our separation from the world enables us to achieve, with the help of the Holy Spirit, exterior and interior quiet, nurturing an integration and harmony of our contemplative life with God, one another and creation in the beauty and wonder of His created world. For this reason the hermitage is established in an area of sufficient acreage and proper solitary location as to safeguard the silence and solitude so necessary for the hermit life.

To insure this we abstain from radio and television. However, mindful of the concerns of the world, several papers and periodicals are available and used with discretion.

SILENCE

"Be still and know that I am God." (Psalm 46:10)

"Silence is the praise that befits Him."
(Psalm 64:1 - Hebrew Version)

Silence is maintained at all times. The Hermits of Bethlehem seek to create for one another an atmosphere of recollection and silence... a silence that is an openness, an awareness of the presence of God within us and creation around us. Silence is essential to the contemplative life. It establishes a consistent movement toward quietness and purity of heart, as well as continual recollection and prayer. It nourishes interior quiet of mind and heart which fosters prayerful union with God. It creates a harmonious rhythm in our hermit life disposing us to receive the gifts of the Holy Spirit. It is by our silence of speech and thought that we speak most truly:

With God (in contemplation)
To God (of others)
Of God (to others)

Far from being a legal silence, our silence is a profound, continual silence that creates a sacred atmosphere where one seeks personal union with God, the core of our life. It is on this Bread of Silence and

Solitude that the Hermit of Bethlehem is nourished and is thus enabled to live in and for God alone.

> **"It is good to wait in silence for the greeting of God... He who sits alone and keeps silence will rise above himself."** (Lamentations 3:26,28)

> **"Thus says the Lord God,**
> **The Holy One of Israel:**
> **By waiting and by calm you shall be saved,**
> **in quiet and in trust your strength lies.**
> **Yet the Lord is waiting to show you favor,**
> **and He rises to pity you;**
> **For the Lord is a God of Justice:**
> **blessed are all who wait for Him!"**
>
> (Isaiah 30:15,18)

Formed in the Womb of Silence

> **"Before I formed you in the womb I knew you;**
> **before you came to birth I consecrated you..."**
>
> (Jeremiah 1:5)

> **"It was You Who created my inmost self,**
> **and put me together in my mother's womb."**
>
> (Psalm 139:13)

As our physical bodies were created and knitted together in our mother's womb, our spiritual beings, our true selves, were formed and are still being formed within the womb of silence.

This formation of the hermit's deepest self is a personal and unique journey with God alone. No one else is privy to your desert itinerary and no one else can make your own personal response to God.

The mysterious reality of this desert experience is the certainty of the transforming power of God's grace within one's being. **"If anyone is in Christ he is a new creation. The old order has passed away; now all is new."** (2 Corinthians 5:17)

The sacredness and beauty of God's transforming power forms the Hermit of Bethlehem in the wisdom of Silence and Solitude.

The hermit enters this sacred stillness where we **"live and move and have our being."** (Acts 17:28) The hermit's life is one of fewer words and becomes one of active listening in one's heart. The realm of the human heart is the sacred meeting place between God and the hermit. Silence is essential to maintain the integrity of the heart. Therefore, this sacred relationship with the Lord is best nourished by silent presence to Him and His Word alone.

Our hidden dialogue with God is a wordless communication and is on a deeper level bringing us into a communion of love with the Lord and so "The Word is Made Flesh in us."

As Jesus was formed in the womb of Mary, we, too, are formed in Jesus in the womb of silence.

DESERT SPIRITUALITY

"The Holy Spirit urged Jesus into the desert..."
(Mark 1:12)

The "desert-wilderness" experience of the hermit, as it is for everyone, is in the realm of the human heart. It puts one in touch with the reality of the false self and the truth of God.

Since the "desert-wilderness" experience depends on an act of faith that the Lord of love is waiting to meet the hermits in "desert" they must first accept the poverty and solitude of their own hearts and be led by Jesus, the Lord of the Desert, to wait and to listen in silence to the gentle Voice of the Holy Spirit and to find therein the forgiving and healing love of the Father.

Through the graced attraction of the Father, the hermit freely chooses to enter this desert, and is thus committed to the inner search. **"Blessed are the single-hearted, for they shall see God."** (Matthew 5:8)

Through the realization of one's sinfulness and consequent spiritual poverty, and as one grows in humility and interior silence the hermit depends on God alone on the journey through this interior desert. It is a call to continual conversion lived in faith, hope and love. Purified by the Fire of the Holy Spirit, the hermit will experience the gradual calming of the passions becoming more and more aware of the presence of God. This interior journey leads to a deeper and more intimate union with God making Him the Absolute of the hermit's life.

Through a vowed eremitical life and public profession of such, the Hermits of Bethlehem consecrate their lives by surrendering all things totally to God. They freely immerse themselves in God's grace and mercy.

God calls the Hermits of Bethlehem to live their lives in solitude given entirely to the love of God and to live for Him alone.

The hermit's first duty is to God, the source of life.

God alone is worthy of all our attention, love, praise and adoration. The hermit seeks solitude not for its own sake, but for God. God is to be loved above all for His own sake. In this way we fulfill God's greatest commandment of love **"...to love Him with all your heart, soul, mind and strength."** (Mark 12:30)

PURITY OF HEART

> **"Blessed are the pure of heart, for they shall see God."** (Matthew 5:8)

The ultimate goal of the eremitical life is the possession of the kingdom of God. **"Seek first His kingship over you, His way of holiness, and all these things will be given you besides."** (Luke 6:33)

The immediate goal of the hermit's desert journey is "purity of heart." It is to will with singleness of purpose one thing, the kingdom of God. Purity of heart is cultivated by giving ourselves completely to the observances of our way of life. It is the asceticism of renouncement of self through the faithful living of the evangelical counsels of poverty, celibate love and obedience.

Purity of heart is living fully in the love of God: love of God for Himself as the supreme goodness and source of all love; love of God in oneself as the beloved child of the Father made to His image; and love of God in our brothers and sisters as we love ourselves, genuinely loving them as Jesus loves us.

Our love for God is real when we love our brothers and sisters. **"We know that we have passed from death to life because we love the brethren. He who**

does not love remains in death." (1 John 3:14) It is wholeheartedly accepting Jesus' invitation: **"If a person wishes to come after me, he must deny his very self, take up his cross and begin to follow in my footsteps."** (Matthew 16:24)

It is living in the Paschal Mystery of Christ that we live a new life. For this reason Jesus came into the world, died and rose again for us. This new life in Christ, this striving for purity of heart, is nurtured through unceasing prayer and docility to the Holy Spirit.

The spirit of the eremitical life is the spirit of Christ Himself: a spirit of humility and love working in the heart of the hermit. Jesus instructs us over and over again: **"Learn of me for I am gentle and humble of heart; your souls will find rest."** (Matthew 11:28) It is the restfulness of the kingdom of God, a foretaste of the heavenly and eternal kingdom.

It is the Holy Spirit of Jesus who leads the hermit into the desert wilderness, purifying and transforming the hermit more and more into the image of God.

The Church has instituted the call of the eremitical life. The hermit freely and humbly responds in love to allow the Holy Spirit to manifest the power and glory of God's grace and His tremendous mercy and marvelous providence.

With deep gratitude we continually offer praise, adoration and thanksgiving to Almighty God in the awareness that our vocation is pure gift. We continually strive for purity of heart by our fidelity to Jesus Christ so that the Holy Spirit will be revealed in us by the gift of His joy and peace.

C. THE BREAD OF PRAYER AND CONTEMPLATION FOUND IN COMMUNION WITH GOD THROUGHOUT THE DAY AND NIGHT

Jesus is our perfect model of prayer. Whether alone or with His disciples He always prayed. His whole life was one with the Father in unceasing prayer. (Matthew 12:25; Luke 10:21; Luke 11:1; Luke 6:12; Mark 1:35 and 6:46; Matthew 4:1 and 14:23)

Our union with God is nourished by the Bread of Prayer. Prayer is our life. Prayer is living in the mystery of God Who dwells in the depths of our being; and Who is also found in our brothers and sisters and in every event and circumstance of life. To pray is to surrender our presence to the presence of God. Prayer is listening to God and responding in love to be and to do His will. God Himself exhorts us to listen and to respond in love to His commandments.

> **"Be careful to listen to all these commandments I enjoin on you, that you and your descendants may always prosper for doing what is good and right in the sight of the Lord your God."**
>
> (Deuteronomy 12:28)

Our prayer is the prayer of Jesus in obedience to the Father for the redemption of the world. On entering the world Jesus said, **"Here I am. I come, God, to do Your will"** (Hebrews 10:9). Jesus gives us His wonderful example of resignation: **"But let it be as You would have it, not as I."** (Mark 14:36)

In prayer we learn what it means to be saved, to be redeemed. We experience the victorious Risen Christ in our being. God touches and transforms us and His presence pervades our consciousness so that He can fulfill His will in us.

Prayer is total dependence on the providence of God as a little child is dependent on its father. Prayer is not the result primarily of our own efforts. Jesus prays in us in His Spirit, and from the innermost recesses of the heart comes the cry, **"Abba, Father."** (Romans 8:15) The prayer of the hermit is a cry from the desert of the heart. It cries of the continual need for conversion and healing.

It is our earnest desire to grow in contemplative prayer by our inner-listening and openness to the Spirit. Often we pray the Our Father: **"Give us this day our daily bread"** (Matthew 6:11). Prayer is our daily bread. Let our hearts always be disposed before the Lord until gradually prayer becomes the atmosphere in which the whole day is lived. We will become the bread of **"unceasing prayer..."** (1 Thessalonians 5:17)

This unceasing prayer is not a mere multiplication of words throughout the day, for our Lord warns against that. It is an attitude of heart, always being attentive to God, whether at rest or at work. Prayer in the life of the Hermit of Bethlehem is not a mere religious exercise. It is the orientation of one's whole life, the breath of one's soul. In becoming hermits, we have chosen to make our whole life a prayer and prayer our life. In this way the hermit fulfills Christ's command: **"...to love God with all your heart, soul, mind and strength."** (Mark 12:30)

This solitary life of prayer and sacrifice unites the hermit with all humankind in the Heart of Jesus. By this life of prayer hidden in the Heart of Jesus in the presence of the Father united in the Love of the Holy Spirit the hermit brings all people to God, and so furthers His kingdom of love, justice and peace revealed in the mystery of the Incarnate Word.

The hermits give themselves to prayer in a spirit of compunction and intense desire. Although we dwell on earth, we are **"intent on the things above rather than on things on earth. After all, you have died! Your life is hidden now with Christ in God. When Christ our life appears, then you shall appear with Him in glory."** (Colossians 3:2-4)

* * * * *

The prayer life of the Hermit of Bethlehem is nourished on the

BREAD OF THE WORD AND THE EUCHARIST

BREAD OF THE WORD

> **"In the beginning was the Word; the Word was in God's presence, and the Word was God."**
> (John 1:1)
>
> **"...the Word became Flesh and made His dwelling among us."** (John 1:14)
>
> **"Not on Bread alone is man to live but on every utterance that comes from the mouth of God."**
> (Matthew 4:4)

The Council Fathers of Vatican II, Constitution of Divine Revelation p. 21, have stated that the Scriptures, the Bread of the Word, are placed on a parallel with the Bread of the Eucharist. Both are sources of spiritual nourishment. The Bethlehem Hermit joins the two forms of Bread, Word and Eucharist, to complete one another. The Council Fathers urge us not just to read but to pray the Scriptures: "Let them remember that prayer should accompany the reading of Sacred Scriptures, so that God and man may talk together, for 'we speak to Him when we pray; we hear Him when we read the divine saying'" (St. Ambrose).

An essential element in the hermit's way of life is Lectio Divina, that is, the attentive, reverent reading of Holy Scripture as the divinely inspired Word of God. This daily practice, relying on the Holy Spirit for insight, leads to prayer (conversation with God), and ultimately friendship with the person of Jesus Christ. The Holy Spirit assures us through Isaiah the Prophet: **"So shall my word be that goes forth from my mouth; it shall not return to me void, but shall do my will, achieving the end for which I sent it."** (Isaiah 55:10,11)

Lectio Divina is the simple action of listening in faith to the Word of God. Reading and praying the Scriptures is a necessary means of being open to God, listening to Him and responding in love. The more completely we engage our energies and faculties, the more deep and enduring our response will be to live the Gospel.

We are to engage the whole person, body, mind, heart, in the practice of Lectio Divina. It involves assimilation of the truths of our faith through discursive meditation, affective prayer, the contemplative experience of savoring the truths of our faith and a personal love of Jesus Christ. In this way our lives are centered on the person of Jesus, the Incarnate Word.

St. Jerome states, "Ignorance of Scripture is ignorance of Christ." Quietly reflecting on the Word of God and allowing it to penetrate our hearts so that it reveals God to us, we will come to have that mind and heart that is in Him, leading us to a closer imitation of Him.

The Sacred Scriptures are at the heart of our daily prayer and a school of contemplation where the hermit speaks with God heart to heart. St. Paul teaches: **"God's word is living and effective, sharper than any two-edged sword. It penetrates the heart and being of a person"** (Hebrews 4:12) and strengthens one's faith, hope and love. At the Liturgy of the Word the hermits' petitions during intercessory prayer are based on the Scriptures of the day.

We find our freedom in God's Word as Jesus promises: **"If you live according to My Word, you are truly My disciples; then you will know the truth and the truth will set you free."** (John 8:31-32)

The hermits will be attentive to the Holy Spirit dwelling within and the Spirit will teach us the meaning of the Word of God for this can awaken a desire in us for God and the things of God.

"Let the Word of God enlighten your mind, strengthen your will and set your heart on fire with the love of God" (Constitution on Divine Revelation, p. 23).

The Bread of the Eucharist

Eucharistic Sacrifice

The Council Fathers of Vatican II teach us: "The Liturgy is the summit toward which the activity of the Church is directed; at the same time it is the fountain from which all her power flows."

(Document of Vatican II on the Liturgy, 10)

The Eucharist is the Sacrament of the Church and therefore, the Sacrament of the hermit. The Eucharist is the living memorial of the Lord's death and Resurrection and the source and nourishment of the contemplative life of the Hermit of Bethlehem.

We draw our life and strength from Eucharist. God gave the Chosen People manna to sustain them in their desert journey to the Promised Land. The manna prefigures Jesus in the Eucharist, the Spiritual Bread by which we are nourished and strengthened in our desert journey to the Heavenly Jerusalem. Jesus proclaimed that He is the true Bread that lasts forever, the **"Bread of God which comes down from heaven, and gives life to the world."** (John 6:32,33)

Jesus invites us: **"If anyone wishes to come after Me, he must deny his very self, take up his cross, and begin to follow in My footsteps. Whoever would save his life will lose it, but whoever loses his life for My sake, will find it"** (Matthew 16:24,25). We can anticipate with great joy that **"...if only we suffer with Him so as to be glorified with Him."** (Romans 8:17)

The Eucharist is the celebration of the Paschal Mystery of Jesus. Jesus said: **"Unless the grain of wheat falls to the earth and dies, it remains just a**

grain of wheat. But if it dies, it produces much fruit." (John 12:24) Jesus is the grain of wheat who fell to the ground and died. Now He is the Risen Lord and the Bread of Life.

By our communion with the Person of Jesus in His sacrifice we are ourselves a gift offered to the Father and we then become bread that is broken for the life of others, for the remission of sins. Nourished on the Bread of the Word and the Bread of the Eucharist, the hermits **"...in their own flesh fill up what is lacking in the suffering of Christ for the sake of His Body, the Church."** (Colossians 1:24)

The Hermit of Bethlehem partakes of the Body and Blood of God's only Son. The life of the hermit is essentially Eucharistic, in that it remains a hidden life, veiled under the appearances of silence and solitude, through which God continually communicates Himself to us, especially in the "Manna of the wilderness." It is through the Eucharistic Heart of Jesus that Love wells up within us, and grows deeper and stronger with each Eucharistic communion until it is perfected in the Paschal Banquet of heaven, where we hope to feast on the vision of God for all eternity.

The hermit lives in this hope of Christ's Eucharistic promise:

> **"He who feeds on my flesh and drinks my blood has life eternal, and I will raise him up on the last day. For my flesh is real food and my blood real drink. The one who feeds on my flesh and drinks my blood remains in me, and I in him."**
>
> (John 6:54-56)

As Eucharist means "thanksgiving," the hermit lives each day in gratitude to God for His many gifts.

> **"Be rooted in him and built up in him, growing ever stronger in faith... and overflowing with gratitude."** (Colossians 2:7)

For these reasons, the Eucharistic Sacrifice is to be celebrated by the hermits every day. It is by sharing in the Paschal Mystery of Jesus that the hermits are bound ever closer to the Lord, to one another and to the whole Church.

Each day at the Eucharistic Celebration, after receiving Holy Communion, 20 minutes are spent in contemplation, before the final prayer and blessing of the Mass.

Eucharistic Adoration

> **"The Father seeks adorers... in Spirit and in truth."** (John 4:23)

The greatest gift from Christ's unconditional love is Himself in the Eucharist.

> **"I myself am the Bread of Life. No one who comes to me shall ever be hungry, no one who believes in me shall ever thirst."** (John 6:35)

The prayer of Eucharistic Adoration is central to the life of the Hermit of Bethlehem.

With the first Shepherds and the Magi united with Mary and Joseph the Hermit of Bethlehem comes before the Eucharistic Lord in silent adoration and homage. The hermits are called by the Holy Spirit to live their lives hidden in the Eucharistic Heart of Jesus in the presence of the Father.

Eucharistic Adoration is the extension of the Eucharistic Sacrifice. In the name of the Church the hermit is a sentinel of adoration and burning love. The hermit's poor prayer is immersed in the Eucharistic Heart of Jesus and is led by the Holy Spirit to offer adoration, thanksgiving, praise, reparation and intercession before our Heavenly Father on behalf of the Church Universal. We pray particularly for our Holy Father, the Bishop of Paterson, all Bishops, Priests, Deacons, Seminarians and Religious. Our prayerful concern, too, is for the sanctity and unity of family life and for those who do not know Christ and all the people of God.

Eucharistic Adoration is prayed one hour in the morning and one hour in the evening in the solitude of the hermitage.

This Eucharistic prayer penetrates our daily work, permeating all of life so that with Jesus we, too, are Bread for one another, for others and the life of the whole world.

Jesus in the Eucharist is God, Who became flesh and dwells among us. It is He Who calls us to solitude. It is He Who will speak to our hearts. He it is Who walks with us in the "desert" of Bethlehem. Without the Eucharist, our life would be lacking the Life of which Jesus Himself said: **"Live on in Me, as I do in you. No more than a branch can bear fruit of itself, apart from the vine, can you bear fruit apart from Me."** (John 15:4)

The Sacraments are the means by which our Lord gives us life. He touches us and gives His life more fully where He already finds it. In the solitude of the desert we need His Life within us, to strengthen and sustain us in this life apart. To live separated from God, especially in His Eucharist, is to be 'dead.'

The hermit strives for constant contact with God through which we allow Christ to become involved in our life. Our desire to encounter Him person to Person means being in contact with His Passion, Death and Resurrection and living His Life.

The Sacrament of Reconciliation

> **"Then he breathed on them and said: 'Receive the Holy Spirit. If you forgive sins, they are forgiven; if you hold them bound, they are held bound.'"**
> (John 20: 22, 23)

The Eucharist leads to Reconciliation, and Reconciliation leads to the Eucharist. When we realize Who it is that we receive in Eucharistic Communion there wells up in us, as did in the centurion, a sense of unworthiness to have the **"Lord enter under my house"** (Luke 7:6), together with sincere sorrow for our sins.

The hermit is aware that one is a sinner like all human beings, and makes every effort with the grace of God to exercise the virtues of faith and humility by claiming the death and Resurrection of Jesus in the Sacrament of Reconciliation. The hermit has been **"led into the desert by the Spirit to be tested"** (Matthew

4:1), that is, like Jesus, to combat evil as it attempts to anchor itself to the soul. It is through the frequent encounter of the Savior through the Sacrament of Reconciliation that the victory is won. It is through the confessional that our sins are washed away in the tide of His Most Precious Blood.

The hermit also exercises penitential discipline to master the body and strengthen the mind and heart in choosing God above the world, the flesh and the devil. In cultivating the virtue of penance, the hermit can stand before God for one's own sake and for the whole world, crying out, **"O God, be merciful to me, a sinner."** (Luke 18:13) Thus the hermit shares with Christ the redemption of humankind.

The perfect gift of the Father's love is His Beloved Son, the "Word made flesh." Jesus came among us with one infinite and burning desire - our *salvation*!

We must always honestly look at ourselves and humbly acknowledge our sinfulness and poverty and with abiding compunction of heart be open to the healing touch of our Lord.

There is nothing that pleases our Blessed Lord more than we humbly acknowledge our sins in true repentance only to receive the embrace of His love and merciful forgiveness.

> **"I tell you, there will be more joy in heaven over one repentant sinner than over ninety-nine righteous people who have no need to repent."**
> (Luke 15:7)

The hermits will receive the Sacrament of Reconciliation at least once or twice a month for it strengthens us in the holiness of God, unites us in the bond of peace and leads us on the way to salvation. Confessors from outside the Laura will be provided for the hermits.

Thus, having changed one's own heart, the hermit can bring forth the **"fruit of the spirit [which] is love, joy, peace, patient endurance, kindness, generosity, faith, mildness and chastity... Those who belong to Christ Jesus have crucified their flesh with its passions and desires. Since we live by the spirit, let us follow the spirit's lead."** (Galatians 5:22,23, 25)

Liturgy of the Hours

> **"I sing your praises, God my King, I bless your name for ever and ever, blessing you day after day, and praising your name for ever and ever. Can anyone measure the magnificence of Yahweh the great, and his inexpressible grandeur?**
>
> **"Celebrating your acts of power, one age shall praise your doings to another. Oh, the splendor of your glory, your renown! I tell myself the story of your marvelous deeds."** (Psalm 145:1-5)

The Liturgy of the Hours is a school of continual prayer and an integral part of the hermit's life. It is prayed in the spirit of the Desert Fathers.

The four-volume Liturgy of the Hours Prayer books, approved by the United States Bishops, are the only books to be used.

This prayer is always the prayer of the Church. When the hermits pray the Liturgy of the Hours, whether in solitude or in common, Christ prays with them and in them. They offer to God a sacrifice of praise, making intercession for the salvation of the whole world. The Hours are prayed at appropriate times according to the Custom of the Hermits of Bethlehem.

The prayer of *Vigils* (Office of Readings) is offered in the hours before sunrise which are appropriately consecrated to God in quiet anticipation of the coming of Christ. For the Hermit of Bethlehem this prayer is made in the solitude of the hermitage. In it, the hermit watches for Christ who promised that He would come back.

> **"The One who gives this testimony says, 'Yes, I am coming soon!' Amen! Come, Lord Jesus!"**
> (Revelation 22:20)

The hermit quietly waits for that coming, mindful of everyone, especially those who struggle in the darkness of temptation and the night of suffering.

At the conclusion of the *Office of Readings* the hermit prays the Memorare in the presence of the Icon of the Mother of the Incarnate Word and prays the aspirations, "Our Lady of Bethlehem, pray for us; St. Joseph, pray for us."

Immediately following the *Office of Readings* the hermit spends one hour in Eucharistic Adoration, concluding with the prayer of consecration to the Heart of Jesus. The hermits then engage in Lectio (Scripture reflection).

The hermits pray *Lauds* (Morning Praise) in the chapel immediately preceding the Eucharistic Liturgy.

> **"From the rising of the sun to its setting may the name of the Lord be praised."** (Psalm 113:3)

The Angelus at midday recalls the hermits from work and other pre-occupations and they pray *Midday Prayer* in the solitude of the hermitage, followed by twenty minutes of contemplative prayer.

Vespers (Evening Praise) is prayed in the solitude of the hermitage and concludes with the Bethlehem Prayer. Immediately following, a hymn in honor of Our Lady (Easter season: the Regina Coeli) is chanted in the presence of the Icon of the Mother of the Incarnate Word followed by the Angelus.

At sunset on Thursdays, commemorating the institution of the Priesthood, the Holy Eucharist and the Mandatum; the hermits gather in the chapel for *Solemn Vespers*. Solemn Vespers includes twenty minutes of contemplative prayer. The Desert Father extends a blessing on each of the hermits taking away the cares and anxieties of the day reconciling each one in the Peace of God and guiding them into the womb of the "nightly silence."

> **"Let my prayer come like incense before you; the lifting up of my hands like the evening sacrifice."**
> (Psalm 141:2)

After *Vespers* the hermits retire in the solitude of the hermitage nourishing themselves with Lectio Divina (Scripture Reading) and spiritual reading.

Finally, *Compline*, the Church's *Night Prayer*, is prayed in solitude just before the hermit retires. In our night prayer we humbly prostrate before our Crucified Lord in repentance (consciousness examen) and gratitude for the blessings of the day. At the conclusion of *Compline* the Salve Regina is chanted as we place ourselves under Mary's maternal care and protection. The Desert Father from his own hermitage extends an evening blessing upon the Laura of hermits.

> **"In peace I lie down, and fall asleep at once, since you alone, Yahweh, make me rest secure."**
> (Psalm 4:8)

The hermits retire by 9:00 p.m., surrendering their spirits into the Hands of the Father Who speaks to their hearts:

> **"With an age-old love I have loved you: so I have kept My mercy toward you... I will place my law within you and write it upon your hearts. I will be your God and you will be My people."**
> (Jeremiah 31:23,33)

D. OUR LADY OF BETHLEHEM: MOTHER OF THE INCARNATE WORD AND OUR MOTHER

> **"I am the servant of the Lord. Let it be done to me as you say."** (Luke 1:38)

After Jesus, Mary, the woman of faith, is the hermit's exemplar in the contemplative life. Like Mary, the hermit strives to be a servant-bearer of the Word by daily:

- opening oneself to the presence and mystery of the Word (Isaiah 50:4)
- listening to and pondering the Word (Luke 2:19)
- believing and treasuring the Word (John 17:20)
- waiting patiently for the Word to take flesh in the

heart through the power of the Holy Spirit (Acts 1:14)
- proclaiming the Word not only by one's speech, but by one's very actions and attitudes of one's life (John 2:5)
- celebrating the Word (Acts 2:46, Luke 4:17,18)
- responding in love to the Word (John 15:23, Mark 3:35)

Through our baptism **"we have died, and our life is hidden with Christ in God"** (Colossians 3:15). As Mary quietly participated in the mystery of God's plan, so, too, the Hermit of Bethlehem is led by the Holy Spirit into the solitude of the heart to live in God's mystery.

Mary's life of presence and openness to God took flesh when she brought forth Christ into the world in the humble cave of Bethlehem. Like Mary, we too, are called to allow Jesus to be born again and again in the cave of our poor, humble hearts.

Mary's joy was manifested through her consent to be the Mother of God. Her joy deepened when she greeted her cousin, Elizabeth, and sang her Magnificat of joy and gratitude because of the deep realization of what God had done for her. **"My spirit finds joy in God, my Savior."** (Luke 1:49)

As Mary rejoiced with infinite joy, not so much for the gifts she received, but in the Source of those gifts - God Himself, we too, are called to echo her deep, spiritual joy. Only when we acknowledge God as the center of our lives will we find that true joy which our hearts seek.

Jesus' words on Calvary to His Mother and the beloved disciple, **"Woman, behold your son... Son, behold your Mother"** (John 19:26,27) encourage the hermit to turn to Mary. Mary, the Mother of the Church, is given to all so that all may grow into the full maturity of Christ.

Mary, Mother of the Redeemer, experienced not only the joys, but the sorrows and sufferings of life. The prophecy of the spirit-filled Simeon was fulfilled in Mary when he said to her: **"This child is destined to be the downfall and the rise of many in Israel, a sign that will be opposed... and you yourself shall be pierced with a sword... so that the thoughts of many hearts may be laid bare."** (Luke 2:34,35) As joy and sorrow are intermingled in life, and as we seek to live the Paschal Mystery, we look to Mary to live our lives as she did, always open to God.

Mary, the first disciple of Jesus, brought the God-Man to the people and the people to God. Like Mary with the disciples in the Cenacle, the hermits continue her mission today through a life of unceasing prayer.

Now the Immaculate Mother enjoys the fullness of her Son's glory and **"all generations will call her blessed."** (Luke 1:48) She who is the Queen of Heaven and our Mother wills only what God wills **"to make known to us the glory beyond price... the mystery of Christ in us, our hope of glory... hoping to make every person complete in Christ."** (Colossians 1:26-28)

The Hermits of Bethlehem look to Mary, Queen of the Desert, to guide them in the journey of the Spirit in a continued Magnificat of praise to the Triune God, that together with her, they will participate fully in the wedding feast of the Risen Lamb. Through her example of selfless love, the hermits seek to live and share Christ's love for the salvation of all.

The Virgin Mary is never absent from the hermit's prayer. The daily recitation of the Rosary is encouraged. Saturdays are dedicated to Our Lady and on that day at the conclusion of the Eucharistic Liturgy a hymn to Our Lady is sung before her icon. Evening Prayer concludes with the "Salve Regina" and during the Easter Season, the "Regina Coeli."

All her liturgical feasts are celebrated with solemnity, in particular the Annunciation of the Lord (March 25th). For we hold this superb creation, Christ's humanity, His manhood taken from Mary, as the marvel of all marvels in which we have our beings. And, because of Mary, He dwells among us and leads us to the fullness of life in the Godhead.

CHAPTER II

The Hermit of Bethlehem will strive to be a living Bethlehem Presence to God in oneself as beloved of the Father

(Integrated Wholeness of Body, Mind and Spirit)

"You shall love your neighbor as yourself."
(Mark 12:28)

"Only when we lose and love ourselves in God can we truly love our brothers and sisters in Christ."
(John 12:25)

In His great love, God created each of us in His image. We are called to deepen our appreciation of this likeness which is a reflection of His love. In this knowledge we will come to know our true self, who we really are, the beloved children of the Father, redeemed by the passion, death and resurrection of His Son.

We are created to be loved and to love. Jesus assures us that we are loveable because we are loved by God and He encourages us to live in His love. **"As the Father has loved me so I have loved you. Live on in My love."** (John 15:9)

While Original Sin has weakened our human nature, making us imperfect and susceptible to temptation and personal sin, all human life in its physical, emotional and spiritual dimensions is fundamentally good.

Christ invites all to live in His Paschal Mystery of the Cross and Resurrection. This involves a change of heart (conversion). In the biblical sense of the word, "Heart" means the whole person (thoughts, feelings, attitudes, desires, emotions). Our goal is to develop the whole person in conformity with the will of God thereby attaining wholeness/holiness in an integrated life of sound intellect, emotions, body, and spirit. This is attained by being nourished in the "Bread of Practical Asceticism."

In the Desert experience of listening to the Heart of Jesus the hermit enters into this continual process of conversion and experience of learning that God loves us, forgives us, welcomes us back and recreates us in His love as our lives are lived wholly hidden in Christ in the presence of the Father.

Depending on the Holy Spirit to help us build rhythms into our daily life that reflect His presence of **"...love, joy, peace, patience, kindness, goodness, gentleness, self-control..."** (Galatians 5:22), we strive for personal growth in the following areas: Body, Mind and Spirit.

THE BODY

"You must know that your body is a temple of the Holy Spirit, Who is within - the Spirit you have received from God. You are not your own. You have been purchased, and at what a price! So glorify God in your body." (1 Corinthians 6:19, 20)

"I beg you through the mercy of God to offer your bodies as a living sacrifice holy and acceptable to God, your spiritual worship." (Romans 12:1)

We must listen to our bodies, giving attention to health, exercise, work, proper diet, fasting and leisure. Because the Holy Trinity dwells within us, making us a "Living House of Bread," we nurture and care for the gift of our bodies and the sacredness of life.

Work

> **"Whatever you do, in word or deed, do everything in the name of the Lord Jesus, giving thanks to God the Father through Him."** (Colossians 3:17)
>
> **"Those who do not work, do not eat."**
> (2 Thessalonians 3:10)

Work is a necessary part of the life of a Hermit of Bethlehem which is a form of asceticism creating a bond of love and unity in the Laura. Work brings the hermit into solidarity with working class persons and is therefore a means of obtaining a livelihood for oneself and others, especially the poor.

Through work, the hermit brings the body under control so as to better attain stability of mind. Having recourse to prayers and aspirations during work can help keep one's mind fixed on God and can often lighten one's work.

Working with one's hands is a way for the hermit to practice humility. The hermit must be careful not to become attached to work by seeking one's self-interest rather than the glory of God.

Work is done in the solitude of one's own hermitage, except when it is necessary for work to be done elsewhere, that is, within the hermitage Laura.

In addition to manual work there is also a variety of other work arising from out of the hermit's state of life especially prayer and divine worship. Under the direction of the Desert Father creative skills are also encouraged. Work unites the hermit to the humble Christ, the workman, Who **"came to serve and not to be served."** (Mark 10:45)

While our primary apostolate is prayer for the salvation of all, we minister to the spiritual and temporal needs of those who come here for the desert experience *according to our spirit of hospitality*. Receiving guests is one of our major means of support.

Leisure

"Come by yourselves to an out of the way place and rest a little." (Mark 6:31)

"Rejoice in the Lord always; again I say rejoice! The Lord is near." (Philippians 4:4, 5)

Besides a time of daily leisure in solitude and silence, the hermit enjoys Sunday, celebrating the glorious Resurrection of the Lord, and Solemnities as days of holy leisure and fraternal joy. On this day there is enough flexibility that will allow, in a family spirit, dinner shared together in the common house while listening to a spiritual tape. It is an opportunity for the hermits to support one another in spiritual discussion and fraternal sharing. There may be other recreational activities, for example, a long walk in the forest, occasional picnics on the property or in another solitary place. This facilitates a mutual rejoicing in our heavenly Father's presence in one another and in creation. It especially fosters a closer bondedness in Christ among the hermits in the Laura.

Meals

> **"Here I stand, knocking at the door. If anyone hears Me calling and opens the door, I will enter his house and have supper with him and he with Me."** (Revelation 3:20)
>
> **"Be like people waiting for their master's return from a wedding, you will open for Him without delay... I tell you, he will put on an apron, seat them at table, and proceed to wait on them."** (Luke 12:35, 36)

Because the Hermit of Bethlehem is called to follow the poor Christ in simplicity of life, meals are simple, yet nourishing. Meatless meals are served frequently.

All meals are taken alone in the solitude of the hermitage. On Sundays and Solemnities, according to ancient eremitical tradition, dinner is shared together in the common house.

All food is prepared in the kitchen of the common house. Each hermit is provided with a food carrier to collect one's meals.

The hermit has a full meal at midday; a light breakfast and optional collation in the evening which is picked up at dinner time. There is no eating in between meals. Water is permissible at all times.

FAST AND ABSTINENCE

The hermit's call to sacrifice, in particular, the sacrifice of fasting, is vital.

Jesus Himself shows us by word and example to fast. Jesus began His public life by a fast of 40 days.

> **"Then Jesus was led into the desert by the Spirit to be tempted by the devil. He fasted forty days and forty nights and afterwards was hungry."**
> (Matthew 4:1-3)

The Hermit of Bethlehem tries to enter into the proper spirit of following Christ, who exhorts us to repent and to take up our cross daily. We do this not only out of obedience to the directives of "Our Way of Life" but mainly to free ourselves from the tendencies of our lower nature and alien spirits within and without so that we will be enabled to follow Our Lord with "purity of heart" more readily. Through God's grace we will be led to the perfection of charity, union with God.

There are times when Jesus exhorts us that **"this kind does not leave but by prayer and fasting."** (Matthew 17:21)

Fasting allows the spirit to dominate the body making us aware of our poverty and total dependence on God. Fasting frees the spirit for prayer.

The Hermit of Bethlehem is mindful that the discipline of fasting can soften the heart unto repentance which leads to compassion. It arouses spiritual desire in one's heart and allows the hermit to share Christ's concern for the hungry, those who hunger for bread and those who hunger for holiness.

Jesus instructs us:

> **"When you fast, you are not to look glum as the hypocrites do. They change the appearance of their faces so that others may see they are fasting. I assure you, they are already repaid. When you fast, see to it that you groom your hair and wash your face. In that way no one can see you are fasting but your Father who is hidden; and your Father who sees what is hidden will repay you."**
>
> (Matthew 6:16-18)

Let our interior and exterior joy, that Christ encourages with fasting, be a sign of the eternal peace and joy He promises.

> **"How can wedding guests go in mourning so long as the groom is with them? When the day comes that the groom is taken away, then they will fast."**
>
> (Matthew 9:15)

We are called to live in the Paschal Mystery. Let us be mindful that after Christ died and left His disciples, the Holy Spirit revealed that we are a pilgrim people "passing over" from this earthly life into the eternal life of blessedness.

Fasting is a process of waiting in sorrow and suffering until the Bridegroom comes and we will "pass over" into all His splendor and glory.

Fasting is observed throughout the year except on Sundays, Solemnities, Christmas Season (Dec. 24 to the Baptism of the Lord) and Easter until Pentecost.

On Ash Wednesday, Good Friday, as well as a weekly Desert Day throughout the year (Wednesday or

Friday) there is a fast on bread and water or some light beverage. Before the final prayer and blessing of the Mass, a ceremony of blessing and anointing with blessed oil prepares the hermit for a day of fast and complete solitude. The hermit is exempt from all work and surrenders oneself entirely to prayer and lectio.

No one is permitted to skip meals or to engage in extra fasting other than observed by our Rule, without the permission of the Desert Father.

If a hermit finds the observance of fasting and abstaining beyond one's strength, an exception can be made with the permission of the Desert Father and in accord with the spirit of sacrifice and penance in our Way of Life.

THE INTELLECT

St. Paul encourages us, **"Let this mind be in you, which was also in Christ..."** (Philippians 2:5) **"Be transformed by the renewal of your mind so that you may judge what is God's will, what is good, pleasing and perfect."** (Romans 12:2) We do this by listening to the ways in which our intellect is informed: study, reading, spiritual direction, prayer and discernment.

The hermit sees study as vital for one's personal growth in the spiritual life.

Lest the hermit wastes time by idleness or deliberate distractions in the hermitage/cell, the hermit must, with discretion, devote oneself to lectio, the study of Sacred Scripture or other fitting studies.

Study is done not for mere curiosity for learning but because wisely-ordered reading endows the mind with greater steadiness and serves as a basis for the contemplation of God and the Word of God.

A bibliography is made available relating to the varied aspects of "The Hermit of Bethlehem's Rule of Life" so the hermits can be intellectually nourished in their vocation.

The Emotions

> God created us **"so that all nations might seek the deity and, by *feeling* their way toward him, succeed in finding Him. Yet, in fact He is not far from any of us, since it is in Him that we live, and move, and exist..."** (Acts 17:27, 28)

We must listen to our feelings, desires, needs, motives, attitudes, in our personal being and in our relationship to others. In dealing honestly with all these, we come to God as human beings with our emotions, fears, anxieties, irrationalities, angers, struggles, temptations, and often sinful tendencies that need healing. Listening to our inner-self is not all darkness, however.

We listen to our feelings by honestly getting in touch with ourselves. We try to get in touch with our feelings by our nightly consciousness examen, our regular meeting with the Desert Father for spiritual direction, in the context of prayer throughout the day and in the Sacrament of Reconciliation with the confessor. Basically, human needs are all the same. It is the duty of the Desert Father to respect and to deal with each hermit on an individual basis because each one has particular needs.

Each hermit will gradually come to discover the beauty and image of God within. We will discover the capacity for love and good. Recognizing our needs, whether intellectual, physical, emotional or spiritual, will make us aware of the needs of others.

THE SPIRIT

"Live in accordance with the spirit and you will not yield to the cravings of the flesh..."
(Galatians 5:13-14)

The hermit is encouraged to listen to one's own spirit and give attention to gospel values necessary for our growth in Christ and conformity to His Holy Spirit by a life of discipline, prayer, the practice of faith, hope and charity and all other virtues.

As we lose ourselves in Christ, we will come to love ourselves in Christ. We will find new life in Him. It will free us to give ourselves wholly to God and to recognize ourselves as beloved children of God. The whole person is to be sanctified.

We are called to love and serve the Lord and one another with our whole heart, mind, body and soul. We believe we can do this to the extent that we seek the Father's will in love.

"Let us love then because He first loved us."
(1 John 4:8)

God takes the initiative to invite us into a loving relationship with Him. We are free to accept or reject that love. When we accept His love and respond to it, we then can love Him with all our heart, mind, soul and strength.

HERMIT SPIRIT

> **"Only in God is my soul at rest, for from Him comes my hope and salvation."** (Psalm 62:1)

The hermit strives to maintain a recollection of spirit, a loving awareness of God's Presence at all times. It is resting in God. It is not only a rest *from* work, but a rest *in* work, that is, the harmonious working of all the faculties and affections of will, heart, imagination and conscience because each has found in God the ideal climate for its satisfaction and development. The hermit spirit is the striving under the guidance of the Holy Spirit for the integration of body, mind and spirit.

Work is done contemplatively in an unhurried ease and in a silence of movement. When it is necessary to speak, it is done softly and briefly.

With humility and ease the hermit carries out all the tasks that a poor and solitary life demands. This is done in such a way that everything is ordered to that ministry of divine contemplation to which the hermit is totally dedicated.

In all work and daily activities the hermit is called to live consciously as a co-creator with God.

> **"May the God of peace make you perfect in holiness. May He preserve you whole and entire, spirit, soul and body, irreproachable at the coming of Our Lord Jesus Christ."**
>
> (1 Thessalonians 5:23)

CHAPTER III

The Hermit of Bethlehem will strive to be a living Bethlehem Presence to God in others as the People of God

(Charity and Hospitality)

In order to be a presence to each other and to our guests, we strive to fulfill the command of Christ:

"to love our neighbor as ourselves." (Mark 12:22)

and to **"love one another as He has loved us."** (John 13:34, 35)

Love Expressed in the Laura

The vocation of the Hermit of Bethlehem is primarily a solitary living out of the response to God's call to holiness. This solitary life is balanced by the encouragement of the hermits, rooted in the love of Jesus.

Through the cultivating of the following, the hermit strives to welcome and accept Christ in one another:

- by a quality of presence, that is, a heightened awareness of the other as person and a child of God, a unique expression of God's love.

- by respectfully listening to what one is saying, not saying.
- by sensitivity to the needs of others.
- by encouraging, supporting and being understanding to others.
- by a loving care given to the sick, so that they will accept their infirmity with patience and for the love of God, uniting their sufferings with Jesus on the cross for the salvation of souls.

Like Mary, the first 'House of Bread' and living tabernacle of Jesus, our desire is to be His peaceful, joyful and loving presence to one another. This can be attained when the spirit of the hermit is nourished on the "Bread of Charity."

Love is very demanding. St. Paul exhorts us to grow in love, for it is the way that surpasses all others (1 Corinthians 13:1-13). Let us be true disciples of Christ by being zealous in the way of love; clothing ourselves with heartfelt mercy, with kindness, humility, meekness and patience. Bear with one another and be mutually forgiving (Colossians 3:12-15). To grow in love, we must not judge others (James 4:11,12). Treat everyone alike. Be merciful to all (James 2:1-13). Jesus calls us to serve instead of being served, in this lies our greatness (Matthew 20:25-28). In this way, we fulfill the new commandment of Jesus: **"Love one another, such as My love has been for you, so must your love be for each other. This is how all will know you for my disciples: your love for one another."** (John 13:34, 35)

> **"May God, the source of all patience and encouragement enable you to live in perfect**

> **harmony with one another according to the spirit of Christ Jesus, so that with one heart and one voice you may glorify God, the Father of our Lord Jesus Christ. Accept one another, then, as Christ accepted you, for the glory of God."**
>
> (Romans 15:5-7)

The Fruit of Charity Is the Bread of Hospitality

Our life of mutual love in this Laura must reflect Christ's love towards our guests. We receive Christ in every guest. Following the Lord's command to love our neighbor and knowing that **"Jesus loved His own to the end... and gave us an example of that utmost love..."** (John 13) we are to be the Bread of Hospitality, that quality of heart which is not what I do for someone but who I am for someone.

Desert hospitality is a welcoming and silent presence. Each guest retreatant is brought into the desert and provided with a hermitage which is nestled in peaceful, wooded surroundings. By the living witness of the hermit's life of prayerful silence and solitude, the guests are gently led into the desert of their own hearts, to grow in love and adoration of the Triune God.

The prayer of silence and solitude becomes an effective door to the healing presence of God in this physical and spiritual environment. An atmosphere of prayer is our gift to our guests. In the spirit of the desert an opportunity for spiritual direction is provided when a spiritual director is available. The Sacrament of Reconciliation is also provided when a priest is available.

We invite clergy, religious and laity (men and

women) into our 'desert' to share our life of solitude, silence and prayer. An atmosphere of prayer is created for our guests, rather than initiating them into a program of prayer.

Hospitality to priests is to be a special focus at Bethlehem. In the charism of their priesthood, priests are called to feed the people of God and in nourishing them we will be nourishing many. Jesus reminds us: **"'Simon, son of John, do you love Me more than these?' 'Yes, Lord', he said. 'You know that I love you.' At which Jesus said, 'Feed my lambs... feed my sheep.'"** (John 21:15-17)

During their stay, whether a weekend or week, the guests are encouraged to share the life of the Bethlehem Hermits.

In order to safeguard our eremitical life of silence, solitude, and prayer, our hospitality to guests must be exercised with discretion. Guests are welcome to our 'desert' provided they abide by our guidelines of the "Hermitage Experience." They are informed of these guidelines beforehand so that they know what is required of them when they come here.

> **"Let us go over to Bethlehem and see this event which the Lord has made known to us. They went in haste and found Mary and Joseph, and the baby lying in a manger; once they saw they understood what had been told them concerning this child."** (Luke 2:15-17)

> **"They were overjoyed at seeing the star, and on entering the house, found the child with Mary His mother. They prostrated themselves and did Him homage."** (Matthew 2:10, 11)

As the angels directed the shepherds to the Child Jesus and as the star led the Magi to bring homage to Christ the King, so may the Bethlehem Hermitage always attract people to silent homage and adoration of Our Lord and Savior.

Strengthened by the healing and renewal that only solitude can bring, the guests go forth like the Shepherds of Bethlehem, **"glorifying and praising God"** (Luke 2:20) and proclaiming His gospel of peace and joy.

CHAPTER IV

A. Introduction to the Vows
Living in the Mysteries of Christ

Consecrated by the Holy Spirit in the Sacrament of Baptism, the hermit is drawn by the Spirit to a closer following of Christ in Obedience, Poverty and Chastity through the public profession of these counsels. It is the same Holy Spirit who **"leads him into the desert"** (Mark 1:12) there to die to self and to the world... disposing the hermit to enter more deeply into the Heart of Jesus.

To be what God wants the hermit to be, that is, to embody in one's own being the mystery of the Incarnate Word in His Childhood (Littleness) is to enflesh humility in its fullness. Humility is the foundation of the spiritual life. Humility is the basis for all the other virtues and, in particular, the foundation for the living out of the evangelical counsels of obedience, poverty and chastity.

Humility depends on self-knowledge leading to the truth. To be humble is to live in the truth. Jesus instructs us, **"I am the Way, the Truth and the Life"** (John 14:6) and again **"...the truth will set you free"** (John 8:32). The hermit acknowledges one's creaturehood and the Creatorship of God. This humility, knowing the true ground of one's being, expresses itself in simplicity, love and childlike trust in the Father.

> **"I assure you, unless you change and become like little children, you will not enter the kingdom of God. Whoever makes himself lowly, becoming like this child, is of greatest importance in the heavenly reign."** (Matthew 18:1-4)

The hermit cannot acquire this humility on one's own. It is a grace from God. Jesus teaches us: **"Take My yoke upon your shoulders and learn from Me for I am gentle and humble of Heart. Your souls will find rest, for My yoke is easy and My burden light."** (Matthew 11:29, 30)

Through the Spirit's graced enlightenment, the hermit sees one's own nothingness and poverty. Like Mary and Joseph, who searched for and prepared a humble place for the Divine Child to be born, the hermit's heart and being are prepared in humility for Jesus to be born again and again, **"for God resists the proud and gives grace to the humble."** (James 4:6)

Coupled with the spirit of childlike trust in the Father, the hermit is invited to follow Jesus more closely in the Paschal Mystery; that is, the poverty of Bethlehem, Nazareth and the Cross, leading to transformation in His glorious Resurrection; to die in order to live so as to give life to others. This is the mystery of the Gospel. Our crosses and joys are transfigured when they are joined to His triumphant Cross and Resurrection. By rising from our own selfishness to concern for others, we share in Christ's Paschal Mystery. The hermit imitates Jesus. **"Your attitude must be that of Christ. Though He was in the form of God, He did not deem equality with God something to be grasped at. Rather He emptied**

Himself and took the form of a slave, being born in the likeness of men. He was known to be of human estate and it was thus that He humbled Himself, obediently accepting even death, death on a cross." (Philippians 2:5-11)

In humility, the hermit's life is centered on God and the hermit lives out that life in a spirit of respectful presence to the mystery of God. We are called to live our life, rooted in the mystery of the Incarnate Word; found in Jesus in the Manger, in Jesus on the Cross and in the empty tomb of His glorious Resurrection. We are drawn and possessed by the mysteries of Jesus. Truly, He continues to come in mystery: **"Of His fullness we have all received, grace upon grace."** (John 1:16)

As disciples of the Risen Jesus, guided by His Holy Spirit, the Hermits of Bethlehem desire to live in the mysteries of Christ's life, flowing from the infinite love of the Triune God: to be poor in spirit, to be little and humble, and to live always in the hope and joy of the Gospel of Jesus. For Jesus prayed: **"Father, Lord of heaven and earth, to You I offer praise; for what You have hidden from the learned and the clever You have revealed to the merest children. Father, it is true. You have graciously willed it so. Everything has been given over to Me by My Father, and no one knows the Father but the Son - and anyone to whom the Son wishes to reveal Him."** (Matthew 12:25-27)

Who can exhaust the unfathomable love and riches of God! Jesus continually calls us to enter deeply into the depths of His love. He invites us to renew His whole mystery in us. Jesus is drawing us to the Father through the gentle power of His Holy Spirit and He desires ardently to live His life in us.

Through the faithful and joyful living of the Vows, the Hermits of Bethlehem freely choose to let Jesus live in them; to let Him pursue His hidden life in them of Bethlehem, Nazareth and Calvary; to be poor in them; to be obedient in them; to love in them; and to pray, sacrifice and labor for souls in and through them so that they can say like St. Paul: **"...and the life I live now is not my own, Christ is living in me."** (Galatians 2:20)

Finally, our Religious Profession of the counsels is a consecration which deepens the consecration initiated by the Holy Spirit in Baptism, and the life of the vows is already an anticipation here below of the life to come. In this regard the life of the hermit, who seeks to live for God above all else, is an anticipation on earth, and thus a sign to the world of that vision of the Triune God, which we long to enjoy for all eternity.

B. THE VOWS: THE FOLLOWING OF CHRIST

By a consecrated religious life of Obedience, Poverty and Celibate Love, we are liberated to give ourselves in a total loving response to Jesus.

The faithful living of the vows will continually kindle the fervor of love (Charity) helping us to live our lives after our only model, Jesus.

Obedience

"My food is to do the will of Him who sent me."
(John 4:34)

"Whoever does the will of my heavenly Father is brother and sister and mother to me."
(Matthew 12:50)

"...religious offer to God a total dedication of their own wills as a sacrifice of themselves" (*Perfectae Caritatis*, 14 - The Documents of Vatican II).

The vow of Obedience frees us to imitate Jesus who sought to be faithful to the Father's will and out of love became obedient even to death on the Cross. **"...and it was thus that He humbled Himself, obediently accepting even death on a cross."** (Philippians 2:8)

In faith and humility we choose to live in loving obedience toward all those who share the authority of Christ (the Holy Father, the Bishop of the Diocese, the Desert Father) and have legitimate authority over the hermits. The one in lawful authority is the instrument of God's will for us. When we obey we must keep our eyes fixed on Jesus. The hermit who acts in obedience out of love receives a blessing from Christ through the Spiritual Father. In doing so we will insure ourselves against dangers, both physical and spiritual, and at the same time, denying our own wills in self-centered judgment.

Our freedom is found in the obedience of Jesus. We believe that our freely accepted obedience joined to Christ's makes our self-emptying love more fruitful because by giving our wills to another, Christ comes within us and gives us His will making us pleasing to the Father. We are not truly free unless we abandon ourselves to God's will, for our holiness is doing God's will.

When we obey those in authority we cooperate in the redemptive work of Christ. The sacrifice of Jesus on the cross was the most perfect act of obedience to the Father's will. Like Jesus, and through Him, we offer to God what is our most precious possession, the sacrifice of our wills.

We show in our lives the effects of the sacrifice of our wills by striving to do His will until our whole life becomes adoration in spirit and in truth. In doing this the perfect prayer of Jesus is fulfilled in us: **"Our Father... hallowed be your name; your kingdom come; your will be done on earth as it is in heaven."** (Matthew 6:9, 10)

Service of Authority

> **"Jesus then called them together and said: 'You know how those who exercise authority among the Gentiles lord it over them; their great ones make their importance felt. It cannot be like that with you. Anyone among you who aspires to greatness must serve the rest, and whoever wants to rank first among you must serve the needs of all.'"**
>
> (Matthew 20:25-26)

The service of authority is exercised by the leader who is called the Desert Father, who serves in imitation of Jesus **"who came not to be served by others but to serve."** (Matthew 20:28) This is to carry the traditions of the early desert spirituality. The Abba (or Amma), Spiritual Father, was the one who gave a word of life. The hermit respects the Desert Father by addressing him as Father. The Desert Father has the awesome responsibility of serving the spiritual needs of those under his care, as well as providing for the temporal needs of the Laura.

We live out our obedience by listening to each other. Therefore, all major decisions are made by the Desert Father in prayer and discernment with the Laura of Hermits. The ultimate decision rests with the Desert Father.

The Desert Father invites an openness with the hermits and respectfully listens to them; and similarly, each hermit is committed to listen to the Desert Father as one would listen to Christ in a spirit of faith.

The Desert Father directs and discerns with the hermits their eremitical vocation through the circumstances, situations, ideas, etc. so that each one will continue to grow in the areas of prayer, work, reading and all the aspects of the Hermit Way of Life.

The Desert Father is to make known to the hermits his concerns and needs of the Laura; he is also to be willing to receive the suggestions of the hermits.

Personal growth is fostered in an atmosphere which blends encouragement with accountability. The Desert Father will have regular interviews with the hermits to discuss how they are progressing in the above areas.

Such a faith relationship is practiced and developed by a regular, one-to-one dialogue between the Desert Father and each hermit in the Laura. Nothing can take the place of this relationship in order to build respect, trust, unity and harmony.

THE DESERT FATHER AND SPIRITUAL DIRECTION

God our Father bestows upon some persons spiritual fatherhood, so that in a spiritual sense new life in the Spirit will be engendered. The desert fathers of the early Church had a unique participation in this God-willed parenthood of the Father.

The spiritual father participates in the regenerating, recreative work of God by awakening and deepening in others the life of the Spirit. Under the guidance of the Holy Spirit, the spiritual father helps hermits and guests discern the movements of the Holy Spirit in their own lives and enables the disciples to experience something of God's own Fatherhood.

This spiritual fatherhood is rooted in Scripture. St. Paul states: **"There is only one God who is Father of all, over all, through all, within all."** (Ephesians 4:6) It is from God alone that all spiritual fatherhood **"whether in heaven or on earth takes its name."** (Ephesians 3:15)

This spiritual fatherhood, which is bestowed by God, is granted so that the disciple can journey to the Father. The role of the spiritual father is to guide, direct and enable the disciple to come into relationship with the Father. The spiritual father first establishes himself in God through prayer, silence and solitude. Then, emerging with the healing presence of God, he is enabled to be for and with others in God's name.

This is not done so much through words or advice, though sometimes this does occur. It is by means of prayer and example that the spiritual fatherhood is communicated.

Insight and discernment, the ability to love others and to make others' sufferings one's own and the power to transform the human environment are basic gifts of a spiritual father. These gifts are given, not for the good of the spiritual father per se, but for the disciple.

The spiritual father helps the disciple to discern between good and evil tendencies, that is, to distinguish the inspirations of the spirit of evil from the spirit of good. Discernment is the means to help the disciple seek and choose what is God's Will. It is guiding the disciple to make right choices to which God is moving the person through the Holy Spirit. The hermit will receive a blessing from God as one who brings **"...into captivity every thought to the obedience of Christ."** (2 Corinthians 10:5)

Doing God's Will is accepting His Kingdom into our hearts and lives. St. Paul reminds us: **"The Kingdom of God is not a matter of eating and drinking, but of justice, peace and the joy that is given by the Holy Spirit. Whoever serves Christ in this way pleases God and wins the esteem of men. Let us then, make it our aim to work for peace and to strengthen one another."** (Romans 14:17-19)

The peace of God is a sign with those who direct their efforts toward what is according to His Will. **"Then God's own peace, which is beyond all understanding, will stand guard over your hearts and minds in Christ Jesus. Finally, your thoughts should be wholly directed to all that is true, all that deserves respect, all that is honest, pure, admirable, decent, virtuous, or worthy of praise. Live according to what you have learned and accepted, what you have heard**

me say and seen me do. Then will the God of peace be with you." (Philippians 4:7-9)

The experience of peace is the awareness that we are being guided by the Spirit. We are aware of His presence and recognize that His Will is leading us.

The spiritual father enables the disciple to see oneself as one truly is and assists the person in discovering the truth for oneself, which brings about one's inner spiritual freedom. He does this, not by teaching his own way, but by instructing the disciple to find the proper way oneself. He acts as God's usher and is not the main character. All the desert father does is meant to guide and direct the disciple to a deeper union with God, helping each one to listen to the Holy Spirit who is the Prime Director of us all.

Two stories are told which typify the role of the desert father. "Abba Theophilus the Archbishop once visited Scetis, and when the brethren assembled they said to Abba Pambo, 'Say something to the Archbishop so that he may be edified.' The old man said to them, 'If he is not edified by my silence, he will not be edified by my speech.'"

Another story is told: "It was the custom of three fathers to visit the Blessed Anthony once each year, and two of them used to ask him questions about their thoughts and the salvation of their souls; but the third remained completely silent, without putting any questions. After a long while, Abba Anthony said to him, 'See, you have been in the habit of coming to me all this time, and yet you do not ask me any question.' And the other replied, 'Father, it is enough for me just to look at you.'"

The desert father is the servant of the Holy Spirit working in the soul of the disciple. Therefore, there is responsibility on the part of both the desert father and the disciple. They both must be praying to be in touch with the Holy Spirit because truly it is the Holy Spirit who guides the soul. The desert father is only an instrument. If either one fails in sincere prayer, there could be no real spiritual guidance and even the danger of being led by our own wills rather than the Spirit of God.

The spiritual father helps the disciple to recognize and to follow the inspirations of grace in one's life in order to reach the end of one's vocation, that is, being formed in the perfect likeness of Christ in God.

Note: The Desert Father/Mother is used alternately with the Spiritual Father/Mother.

Poverty

> **"If you wish to be perfect, go and sell what you own and give the money to the poor, and you will have treasure in heaven; then come, follow me."**
> (Matthew 19:21)

> "Poverty voluntarily embraced in imitation of Christ provides a witness which is highly esteemed... shares in the poverty of Christ... should banish all undue solicitude and trust themselves to the provident care of their Father in heaven" (*Perfectae Caritatis*, 13).

The Hermits of Bethlehem respond in love to follow the call of Christ in a life of poverty. Unless the hermit experiences the riches of Christ's love, the hermit cannot be poor with Christ and possess the Kingdom. The hermit strives to be open to the experience of God's love, that is, with one's whole being. One must know that one is loved by God and that there is a growing relationship with God. It is not the law, but the experience of His love that enables the hermit to turn away from the possessions of the world and give attention to God.

For Jesus encourages us: **"Do not lay up for yourselves an earthly treasure... Make it your practice instead to store up heavenly treasure... Remember, where your treasure is, there your heart is also... I warn you, then: do not worry about your livelihood, what you are to eat or drink or use for clothing. Is not life more than food? Is not the body more valuable than clothes?**

Look at the birds in the sky. They do not sow or reap, they gather nothing into barns; yet your heavenly Father feeds them. Are you not more important than they?... Learn a lesson from the way the wild flowers grow. They do not work; they do not spin... If God can clothe in such splendor the grass of the field, will he not provide much more for you, o weak in faith!

Your heavenly Father knows all that you need. Seek first his kingship over you, his way of holiness and all things will be given you besides. Enough, then, of worrying about tomorrow. Let tomorrow take care of itself. Today has troubles enough of its own." (Matthew 6:19-34)

The vow of poverty liberates us to imitate joyfully and willingly the poor and humble Jesus of Bethlehem, of Nazareth and of Calvary. The meeting place of the Lord is in the poverty of our hearts; seeing our own littleness and total dependence on Him Who transforms us. Our truest identity is found in Jesus. By losing our life in Him we shall find new life: **"Happy are the poor in spirit; theirs is the kingdom of heaven."** (Matthew 5:3)

By the vow of poverty the hermit makes a public renunciation of the possession of material goods. Voluntary poverty frees us from worries and anxieties and helps us to be dependent on our heavenly Father Who provides for all our needs. By owning nothing for the sake of Jesus, we possess All.

Our vow of poverty emphasizes our dependence on our Provident Father which is understood to include dependence on one another. Our vow focuses on poverty of the heart which instills in the hermit a spirit of willingness to accept whatever level of simple living God chooses and allows to provide through the work of our hands, the work with guests who come for the desert experience, the Spiritual Union of Our Lady of Bethlehem, donations for art work, etc.

The vow of poverty opens the hermit to a simplicity free from the distractions of excessive possessions or abject poverty. The ideal of the Hermit of Bethlehem is to strive in a spirit of detachment to live by the fundamental principle: How free am I in my relationship with God that in the poverty of my heart, I am so dependent on God that He can make the choices for me? The hermit will practice holy indifference, allowing oneself to be free to have or not to have, that is, never to be attached to anything, but God alone.

Poverty of spirit is to be forgetful of self with one's gaze always fixed on Jesus, for Jesus instructs us: **"No one who puts his hands to the plow and looks back is fit for the kingdom of God."** (Luke 9:62) Looking back is trying to possess things, persons, having control, etc. and thereby one loses simplicity of heart. Jesus exhorts us: **"He who loves his life, loses it and he who hates his life in this world will keep it for eternal life."** (John 12:25)

It is the poverty of a truly consecrated and immolated heart that the hermit can find oneself and truly love oneself. It is here we find our identity in Jesus and reflect the image of the Father.

The hermits pray for the grace of self-emptying to accept always our poverty of spirit, for in this way the hermit can be truly dedicated to God for the sake of His kingdom and will be able to make every sacrifice according to God's Will.

Poverty of spirit invites us to accept whatever discomfort and privations the Father sends and allows for the love of Jesus Who made Himself poor to make us rich. By our vow of poverty we freely choose simplicity in fact and in spirit with the poor Christ, and thus become one with those who are involuntarily poor. This simplicity witnesses by the very life of the hermit total dependence on God and the desire for Him to be our All.

Mindful of the poor, the hermits not only pray for, but share with the needy and the poor. It is our spirit to welcome as our guests those who minister to the poor so they can be renewed and strengthened. Jesus encourages us: **"Whatever you do for the least of mine, you do for me."** (Matthew 25:40)

The Hermit of Bethlehem's vow of poverty is the renunciation of all possessions and also the surrender of one's own body and will in the service of God. The hermit is called to greater simplicity, and therefore is to possess nothing as one's own. In all necessities the hermit makes oneself available to and dependent on the Laura and requires the permission of the Desert Father for the fulfillment of one's needs.

It is the free surrender of the goods of the world that is praiseworthy, not deprivation or destitution. Our goal is **"contentment with sufficiency"** (1 Timothy 6:6): a great simplicity of life, that is, the reduction of needs and a rejection of anything that is excessive and unnecessary without at the same time confusing ugliness with poverty.

The hermit appreciates the simple beauty of God's creation, especially in our space of worship (the chapel) that lifts our minds and hearts in prayer of praise, adoration and thanksgiving to God.

In living our life of poverty we are careful that poverty does not become an idol and an end in itself so that it does not become detrimental to a wholistic way of spirituality. Evangelical poverty is a necessary means to union with God. In this way the hermit hopes to give witness to the presence of God's peace, joy and loving Providence.

CELIBATE LOVE
(*CHASTITY*)

"I should like you to be free of all worries. The unmarried man is busy with the Lord's affairs, concerned with pleasing the Lord..."

"The virgin, indeed, is concerned with things of the Lord, in pursuit of holiness in body and spirit..." (1 Corinthians 7:32-34)

"Chastity liberates the human heart in a unique way and causes it to burn with a greater love for God and all mankind" (*Perfectae Caritatis*, 12 - The Documents of Vatican II).

The vow of Celibate Love frees us from our own selfishness and intensifies our desire to love God above all things. The more we love God, the more we are free to love ourselves and our brothers and sisters. By living out our vow of chastity, cheerfully and without compromise, we will allow the love of Jesus to flow into ourselves and through us to others.

By our vow of chastity we become a sacred vessel consecrated solely for God. We become the property of Christ, whereby our souls are wedded to Him in undivided love, nurtured on the Bread of the Word and consummated in the Eucharist, making us one with the Heart of Jesus and into the very Heart of the Trinity.

Celibacy is a gift of God. Knowing that we carry this treasure, a pearl of great price, in earthen vessels the hermit asks for the grace to strive daily for a genuine esteem and respect for all those with whom we live and whom we serve. It is to have a genuine concern for the other and not for oneself. This is expressed in a welcoming attitude, kind and gentle words, quiet attention to others' needs, and striving for mastery of emotions, thoughts and imagination. The hermit does this under the protection of the Virgin Mary and her chaste spouse Joseph.

It is in the light of the Nativity of Jesus in Bethlehem, His hidden life in Nazareth and His death on Calvary that we can plumb somewhat the depth of Christ's love, obedience, humility, poverty, purity of heart and the way of simplicity and spiritual childhood. (Christ made the way of childlikeness the absolute condition to enter the Kingdom of Heaven.)

It is the contemplative's particular way of following Jesus in love. The Hermit of Bethlehem is called to live a life hidden in Jesus in all His mysteries, that is, a life of loving obedience, poverty and celibate love. Our living of the evangelical counsels must be motivated by love, so that all that we do is done out of love for God: love of God for His own sake, love of God in ourselves as beloved children of the Father and love of God in our brothers and sisters as Christ loves.

C. CONSECRATED LIFE IN THE CHURCH

The Second Vatican Council in her *Constitution on the Church* says that the Church is a community of God's people, the Bride of Christ. The Church belongs to Christ because it was founded by Jesus Christ upon the Apostles.

Through the grace of our Baptism we have become a new people redeemed by the Most Precious Blood of Christ making us sons and daughters, fellow citizens with the Saints and members of God's household.

As members of the Church, we are united to Christ, the Head, in His Mystical Body, vivified by the Holy Spirit bringing us to the Father. We live in the Church and must live with the Church.

As sons and daughters of the Church, we pledge our loyalty and obedience to the Holy Father, the Vicar of Christ on earth, to the magisterium of the Church, to the local Ordinary, the Bishop of the Diocese. We wholeheartedly embrace the inspired words of Scripture:

> **"Obey your leaders and submit to them, for they keep watch over you as men who must render an account. So act that they may fulfill their task with joy, not with sorrow."** (Hebrews 13:17)

A LITTLE CHURCH

The Laura, or the hermit as an individual, could be considered an Ecclesiola, a little Church. For, as St. Paul states: **"There are many gifts but one Spirit — and the gifts of the Holy Spirit are given for the benefit of the whole body."** (1 Corinthians 12:4,7) The hermit, a gift of the Holy Spirit to the Church, lives not only in communion with others, but in the mystery of the Church and in God, and a life of love expressly lived for others.

Love of neighbor not only refers to external deeds of charity, but it also refers to the interior life of prayer, a life hidden in Jesus before the Father for the "salvation of the world" (Canon 603).

The Church sees the importance of the hermit vocation for she states in the recent Code of Canon 603: "Besides institutes of consecrated life, the Church recognizes the life of hermits or anchorites, in which Christ's faithful withdraw further from the world and devote their lives to the praise of God and the salvation of the world through the silence of solitude and through constant prayer and penance."

"Hermits are recognized by law or dedicated to God in consecrated life if, in the hands of the diocesan bishop, they publicly profess, by a vow or some other sacred bond, the three evangelical counsels, and then lead their particular form of life under the guidance of the diocesan bishop." (Canon 603)

Pope Paul VI expressed to a group of contemplative hermits his admiration and importance of their hidden life in the Church..."You are here very close to the Lord, dedicated to His service... You have left the world with all its seductions and vanities, and you have also renounced that which is good, beautiful and lawful - such as the apostolate for souls - and all this is so that you might enclose yourselves in this holy place in order to attend wholly to prayer... You have the great mission of animating all these works of ours... although you have sacrificed the desires of an external apostolate, you are by no means on the fringe of the Church, but you are in the very center of the Church, close to the Heart of God."

CHAPTER V

Formation: Transformation Into Christ

Each person who seeks to be a Hermit of Bethlehem must already be somewhat formed in the spiritual life and should have attained a certain level of maturity. Before entering the solitary way of the Hermits of Bethlehem, a seeker must first have been tested and tried in some form of communal way of life. The seeker would have to complete successfully a pre-entrance program, as defined in our Statutes, to discern one's openness to grow and become rooted in the ways of God. Each candidate must give evidence that one is able to assume the hermit way of life here at Bethlehem with a fiexibility which always seeks solitude and is faithful to a life of prayer.

The purpose of formation is to help the candidate to understand and to live the rule and spirit of life as a consecrated Hermit of Bethlehem of the Heart of Jesus and to grow in union with God.

Pre-Entrance

When a candidate applies for admission to us, careful inquiries are made by the Desert Father regarding the background as well as the physical, mental, emotional and spiritual health of the candidate. This is done by brief encounters with the Desert Father (through correspondence, retreats, visits and questionnaires).

Previous to the three-month live-in, the seeker will be required to participate in a program of psychological testing recommended by Bethlehem.

PROSPECTIVE CANDIDACY

There will be suitable times (including at least a three month "live-in") for the candidate to observe and be observed as to the qualities essential for the human, emotional and spiritual maturity.

This affords the potential candidate to experience first-hand, the life of the Bethlehem Hermit. During these times, the candidate's motives and aptitudes will be carefully evaluated.

There must be clear and hopeful signs that the candidate will be capable of assuming the full obligations of the eremitical life of the Hermits of Bethlehem.

At the end of the "live-in" the pre-candidate will leave the Laura for a short period of time arrived at in consultation with the Desert Father, after which the pre-candidate may apply by letter to be accepted as a candidate.

FORMATION

Candidacy

Candidacy will include:

1. Introduction to the Rule and charism of the Hermits of Bethlehem of the Heart of Jesus, as well as its historical development
2. Spiritual direction by the Desert Father
3. Development of the prayer and spirit of our Way of Life (Eucharistic Adoration, Prayer in Solitude, Liturgy of the Hours, etc.)
4. The study, appreciation and participation in the Liturgical Eucharistic Sacrifice around which our day revolves
5. Acclamation to and integration of prayer and work

After a period of nine to twelve months, candidates may request by letter to the Desert Father for admission into the Novitiate.

Religious Habit

At the beginning of the novitiate, the candidate receives the habit. The Hermits of Bethlehem wear a blue-grey habit made up of a tunic and scapular and a black belt. The hermit brother wears a hood attached to the scapular. The hermit sister wears a blue-grey veil while the novice wears a white veil. Over the scapular a simple wooden cross on a leather cord is worn. The novice wears a white cape during the liturgical services.

The candidate sister wears a blue skirt or jumper and the brother wears a blue-grey shirt with hood.

At the ceremony of perpetual profession a white cowl, symbol of the hermit's perpetual consecration, is presented to the hermit to be worn at all liturgical functions and during prayer in the solitude of the hermitage. The hermit also receives the Profession Crucifix.

NOVITIATE

Novitiate will include:

1. History of spirituality
2. Prayerful study of Sacred Scripture
3. Ongoing spiritual direction
4. More in-depth study of contemplative prayer and the charism of the Hermits of Bethlehem of the Heart of Jesus
5. The study and practice of Christian Asceticism in order to grasp and appreciate the potentials of the human person in an integrated life of sound mind, body and spirit
6. The writings of the Fathers of the Church, especially the Desert Fathers and Mothers
7. The Encyclicals of the Church, in particular the Documents of the Second Vatican Council and the pastoral letters of the American Bishops
8. Pertinent documents of the Church of Paterson

Temporary Vows

After a novitiate of two years, which may be extended by the Desert Father for up to one year, a novice not already professed in perpetual vows in another Institute, may request by letter to the Desert Father to take temporary eremitical vows of obedience, poverty and chastity in the hands of the Bishop and in the presence of the Desert Father in accordance with Canon 603 and the Statutes of the Association. Temporary vows will be renewed annually up to three years in a private ceremony. In preparation for temporary and final vows the hermit will spend eight days in solitary retreat under the guidance of the Desert Father.

Permanent Vows

After three years the hermit in temporary vows may request by letter to the Desert Father to take perpetual vows and enter into permanent membership in the Association.

After a probationary time of two years, which may be extended by the Desert Father for up to one year, a religious already professed in perpetual vows in another Institute, may request by letter to the Desert Father to enter into permanent membership in the Association by the profession of final vows. These final vows are received by the Bishop of the Diocese. An indult of departure from the former Institute must be obtained prior to perpetual vows in the Association.

Ongoing Formation

There will be a continual updating and renewal of religious life, seeking a balance and harmony between the living tradition of the Church and necessary changes in the Church and Society postulated by the signs of the times.

In the spirit of the Desert Fathers the hermit will meet on a regular basis with the Desert Father for spiritual guidance.

Renewal of Vows

On the anniversary of final profession the individual hermit and on the Feast of the Annunciation of the Lord the Laura of hermits will renew their vows after the Liturgy of the Word at the Eucharistic Liturgy preceded by a day of total solitude.

Daily Horarium of the Hermits of Bethlehem

"And rising up long before daybreak, He went out and departed into a desert place, and there He prayed." (Mark 1:35)

Pre-dawn — The day of desert spirituality for the Hermits of Bethlehem begins.

The hermit engages in the listening Office of Readings (Vigils) in the solitude of the hermitage, which includes readings from Scripture and the early Church Fathers and praying the psalms in the spirit of the Desert Fathers. After Vigils the Memorare is prayed in the presence the Icon of the Mother of the Incarnate Word.

In the solitude of the hermitage the hermit is nourished by one hour of Eucharistic Adoration, concluding with the prayer of consecration to the Heart of Jesus.

Dawn — The hermits engage in Lectio (Scripture reflection) in the solitude of the hermitage.

"From the rising to the setting of the sun is the name of the Lord to be praised." (Psalm 113:3)

Sunrise — The bell is rung announcing the Mystery of the Incarnation and each hermit prays the Angelus silently.

Lauds (Morning Praise) is prayed in chapel. Immediately following Lauds the Eucharistic Sacrifice is celebrated and is the heart of the hermits' day. From this living Source, the hermits draw strength to live their eremitical life. There are 20 minutes of contemplative prayer after communion concluding with the final prayer and blessing of Mass.

A simple breakfast is taken in the solitude of the hermitage.

Morning — Assigned work, spiritual direction with the Desert Father, studies and conferences are undertaken.

"Whatever you do, whether in speech or in action, do it in the name of the Lord Jesus. Give thanks to God the Father through Him." (Colossians 3:17)

Midday — The Angelus is prayed.
Dinner is taken as the hermit dines intimately with the Lord.

"Here I stand, knocking at the door. If anyone hears Me calling and opens the door, I will enter his house and have supper with him and he with Me." (Revelation 3:20)

After dinner there is personal leisure time.

In the solitude of the hermitage Midday Prayer is prayed, including 20 minutes of contemplative prayer.

Afternoon — The hermits are involved in assigned work, study or creative skills in the hermitage.

Evening — The hermits surrender themselves to God in an hour of solitary prayer in the hermitage.

Sunset — Vespers, the Evening Prayer of the Church, is prayed in the solitude of the hermitage. But on Thursdays, commemorating the institution of the Priesthood, the Holy Eucharist and the Mandatum, the hermits gather in the chapel for Solemn Vespers, which includes 20 minutes of contemplative prayer.

Upon the conclusion of Vespers the Bethlehem Prayer is said and a hymn to Our Lady (Easter season: the Regina Coeli) is chanted in the presence of the Icon of the Mother of the Incarnate Word, followed by the

Angelus. The Desert Father extends a blessing on each of the hermits, taking away the cares and anxieties of the day, reconciling each one in the Peace of God and guiding them into the womb of the "nightly silence."

> **"Let my prayer come like incense before You; the lifting of my hands like the evening sacrifice."**
> (Psalm 141:2)

Following Vespers there is an optional light collation and some leisure time in the solitude of the hermitage. The hermits also nourish themselves with Lectio and spiritual reading.

Night

Consciousness Examen and Compline, the Church's Night Prayer, are prayed in the solitude of the hermitage. At the conclusion of Compline the Salve Regina is chanted as we place ourselves under Mary's maternal care and protection.

> **"In peace I lie down and fall asleep at once, since you alone, Yahweh, make me rest secure."**
> (Psalm 4:8)

The hermits retire, surrendering their spirits into the Hands of the Father Who speaks to their hearts:

> **"With an age-old love I have loved you; so I have kept My mercy toward you... I will place My law within you and write it upon your hearts. I will be your God and you will be My people."**
> (Jeremiah 31:23, 33)

DESERT DAY

"The Holy Spirit urged Jesus into the desert..."
(Mark 1:12)

The hermits participate in a weekly Desert Day. Before the final prayer and blessing of the Mass a ceremony of the blessing of bread and anointing prepares the hermits for a day of fast and complete solitude. The hermit is exempt from all work and surrenders oneself entirely to prayer and lectio.

SUNDAY

"This is the day the Lord has made; let us rejoice and be glad." (Psalm 118:24)

Sunday, because of its Association with the glorious Resurrection of Our Lord, is a day of fraternal joy and holy leisure.

On this day dinner is taken together in the Common House, while listening to a spiritual tape. This is an opportunity for the hermits to share with and support one another. There may be other recreational activities, for example, a long walk in the forest.

Solemnities are also occasions for fraternal joy and holy leisure.

EPILOGUE

The Bread of Peace

As we approach the third millennium of Christianity we are moved to reflect briefly on its beginnings.

Two thousand years ago the little town of Bethlehem awoke to the gentle and awesome presence of the Prince of Peace - Jesus Christ: **"God so loved the world that He gave His only begotten Son..."** (John 3:16), an unparalleled gift of salvation.

"Peace and Light" broke the stillness and darkness of the night. Peace - a word that is the very essence of the first Christmas message. It was peace for which He had been sent to give; and it was peace that would mark not only the beginning of His earthly life, but also the end as well. At His birth the angels sang: **"Peace on earth to those on whom His favor rests."** (Luke 2:14)

After His death He arose and appeared to His disciples, greeting them with: **"Peace be with you... As the Father has sent me, so I send you."** (John 20:21)

There is a longing in every human heart for peace, inner peace. In contrast to the peace and joy of Bethlehem, we read and hear about so much unrest in the hearts of people and in the world.

The Desert Fathers regarded a society without the love of Christ as a shipwreck from which each single person had to swim for one's life. They believed that to let oneself drift along, passively accepting the values of their society, was simply a disaster.

The world offers vain solutions for its problems today. The words of Jeremiah ring true:

> **"They have healed the wounds of my people lightly, saying, 'Peace, peace' where there is no peace. Were they ashamed when they committed abomination? No, they were not at all ashamed. They did not know how to blush... but there is hope in the Lord Who says, 'Stand by the roads, and look, and ask for the ancient paths, where the good way is; and walk in it, and find rest for your souls...'"** (Jeremiah 6:14-16)

The Hermits of Bethlehem hear the cries of God's people for healing and peace through the many requests for prayers. But what is peace? Peace is not just mere passivity or some good feeling. Peace is a gift of Jesus and a fruit of the Holy Spirit. In the words of St. Augustine: "Peace, that magnificent gift of God, even understood as one of the fieeting things of earth, no sweeter word is heard, no more desirable wish is longed for, and no better discovery can be made than this gift."

Peace comes from our being open to the tremendous love of God, in the Gift of the Incarnate Word. **"God so loved the world that He gave His only begotten Son..."** (John 3:16). As children of the Father, we can respond in loving obedience to His commandments and by living His Gospel teachings. This is something for which we all have to work and strive.

Peace is God's gift to us. The Hermits of Bethlehem are to be His presence and quiet messengers of peace to one another and to promote it in the society in which we live. In the words of John Paul II: "The Church supports and encourages all serious efforts for peace. It unhesitatingly proclaims that the activity of all those who devote their energies to peace forms part of God's plan for salvation in Jesus Christ."

What does "the best of our energies" mean? The Bishops of the United States in the Pastoral Letter, "The Challenge of Peace," stated it as follows:

> "A conversion of our hearts and minds will make it possible for us to enter into a closer communion with our Lord. We nourish that Communion by personal and communal prayer, for it is in prayer that we encounter Jesus, Who is our peace and learn from Him the way of peace.
>
> "We are called to be peacemakers not by some movement of the moment but by our Lord Jesus Christ... The practice of contemplative prayer is especially valuable for advancing harmony and peace in the world. For this prayer rises, by divine grace, where there is total disarmament of the heart and unfolds in an experience of love which is the loving force of peace.
>
> "Contemplation fosters a vision of the human family as united and interdependent in the mystery of God's love for all people."

The Bethlehem Hermitage is to be an oasis of peace. We, the Hermits of Bethlehem. guided by the light of Jesus, are to be opened to His continual call, dedicating ourselves to live our eremitical lives more deeply hidden in the Eucharistic Heart of Jesus so that before the Father and in the power of the Holy Spirit we may be transformed more and more as servants of His Gospel of peace and love. Nourished on the Bread of the Word and Reconciliation and the Bread of the Eucharist, we shall be the Bread of Peace.

In this environment of prayer in the silence of solitude we invite the clergy, religious and the laity to experience the gift of God's peace so that they in turn may be Christ's presence of peace in the challenges of the world in which they live.

St. Paul encourages us: **"Rejoice in the Lord always! I say it again. Rejoice! Everyone should see how unselfish you are. The Lord is near. Dismiss all anxiety from your minds. Present your needs to God in every form of prayer and in petitions full of gratitude. Then God's own peace, which is beyond all understanding, will stand guard over your hearts and minds, in Christ Jesus. Finally, your thoughts should be wholly directed to all that is true, all that deserves respect, all that is honest, pure, admirable, decent, virtuous, or worthy of praise. Live according to what you have learned and accepted, what you have heard me say and seen me do. Then the God of peace will be with you."** (Philippians 4:4-9)

Bethlehem Prayer

Jesus, gentle and humble of Heart, You are the Bread of Life; help me to live my life hidden in Your Eucharistic Heart in the Presence of our Father united in the love and power of Your Holy Spirit.

Give me a listening heart, a heart to love You for Your own Sake, to love You in myself, and to love You in my brothers and sisters as You have loved.

Consume me in the fire of Your Love.

Mary, Mother of the Incarnate Word and my Mother, you are the first "house of bread."

Help me to live in perfect love by being:
the bread of Humility and Abandonment to the Father's Will;
the bread of Purity of Heart;
the bread of Word and Eucharist;
the bread of Simplicity, Poverty and Littleness;
the bread of Silence and Solitude;
the bread of Prayer and Contemplation;
the bread of Reconciliation and Peace;
the bread of Interior and Joyful Suffering;
the bread of Charity and Hospitality, broken and offered with Jesus to the Merciful Father and shared for the salvation of the world.

Holy Mary, Lady of Bethlehem, Queen of the Desert, guide me in the journey of the Spirit that, together with you, I may participate in the wedding feast of the Risen Lamb until at last I may sing an eternal Magnificat of Love and Praise face to Face before our All-Holy Triune God. Amen.

Statutes of The Hermits of Bethlehem of the Heart of Jesus of the Diocese of Paterson in Chester, New Jersey a Public Association

I
PURPOSE

The Hermits of Bethlehem of the Heart of Jesus is an eremitical contemplative Public Association of Catholic men and women approved and erected by the Bishop of the Diocese of Paterson and is under his ecclesiastical authority. It is primarily a solitary living out of the response to God's call to holiness, living in intimate union with God, balanced by the support of the hermits.

So as to insure a stricter separation from the world, the hermits do not engage in the active apostolate. This enables the hermits to respond in love to a life of assiduous prayer, penance and the silence of solitude for the praise of God and for the salvation of the world (Canon 603).

II
WAY OF LIFE

The members of this Association, living as a Laura, that is, hermits dwelling in separate, solitary hermitages around a central chapel and common house, are united in the love of the Heart of Jesus and the Heart of the Church under the protection of Mary, Mother of the Incarnate Word and our Mother. The hermits live in obedience to the Desert Father/Mother who, in imitation of Jesus, serves the brothers and sisters.

The spirituality of the Hermits of Bethlehem is based on the Gospel of Jesus Christ as lived in the spirit and teachings of the Desert Fathers and Mothers of the early Church.

III
GUESTS

The hermits receive Christ in every guest. Hospitality is a welcoming and silent presence. The hermits invite priests, religious and the laity into the "desert" to share their life of solitude, silence and prayer for a period of time, so as to experience the healing process of God in this spiritual and physical environment. Through the welcoming and silent presence of hospitality and by the living witness of the hermits to the hidden **and desert life of Jesus, the guests are gently led into the desert of their own hearts to grow in love and adoration of the Triune God.**

IV
EREMITICAL VOWS

In living out the life of the Hermit of Bethlehem a permanent member will take public perpetual vows of

Obedience, Poverty and Celibate Love (Chastity) in the hands of the local Ordinary and in the presence of the Desert Father according to Canon 603 and the Way of Life of the Hermits of Bethlehem of the Heart of Jesus in order to follow Christ more perfectly.

+ Obedience

In faith, the hermit chooses to live in loving obedience to the Holy Spirit within and toward all those who share the authority of Christ (the Holy Father, the Bishop, the Desert Father) and have legitimate authority over the hermits. In imitation of Jesus, and through Him, we offer to God what is our most precious possession, the sacrifice of our own wills. In this way we cooperate in the redemptive work of God.

+ Poverty

The hermit gives up radically the right to use possessions so that the hermit will be rich in the possession of God and give witness to the Presence of God's peace, joy and loving Providence.

+ Celibate Love (Chastity)

By the vow of chastity, the hermit gives up radically the right to marriage and lives in perfect continence in order to allow the love of Jesus to flow into ourselves and through us to others.

V
ADMINISTRATION

+ HERMITAGE GOVERNMENT

The Association will be governed by a spiritual moderator called the Desert Father (or Desert Mother), appointed by the bishop. Initially, the founder, who is the first permanent member, will serve as the Desert Father. At such time as the founder is no longer capable of acting in this capacity or for some other serious cause as determined by the bishop, a Desert Father will be appointed by the bishop from among the perpetually professed hermits, for a term of three years, which may be renewed only once.

The Association is approved and erected by the Bishop of Paterson and subject to him according to the norms of Canon Law. The Desert Father acts in legal matters in the name of the Association. As such, the Association is subject to the norms of Canon Law.

+ BOARD OF ADVISORS

A Board of Advisors, composed primarily of lay persons, will exist to advise on matters involving development of physical property, finances, legal issues and other appropriate matters. The role of the Board of Advisors is advisory and consultative. It is never related to internal acts of governance or policy.

+ Meetings and Decisions

The Desert Father invites an openness with the hermits (both provisional and permanent members) by conducting regular meetings and respectfully listening to the hermits. All major decisions are made by the Desert Father in prayer and discernment with the membership. The Chapter Members are comprised of perpetually professed hermits. The statutes will be reviewed yearly. Changes are made in consultation with the Chapter Members. They are submitted to the bishop for approval.

+ Work

All the hermits share in the responsibility of work (maintenance, domestic, secretarial, etc.) which is done in solitude.

+ Finances

1. All the hermits will execute a signed agreement upon entering the Laura that the Association is not obligated to make remuneration for work done while living in the Laura. Any earnings resulting from work performed by the hermits while living in the Laura will become the property of the Association. (Canon 668, paragraph 3)
2. The temporal needs of the hermits while living in the Laura will be supplied by the Association.
3. Gifts given to members of the Association are placed in the common fund.
4. Hermits will be responsible for their own medical bills until they become permanent members.

5. While retaining ownership, at the time of temporary profession, members in the Laura will cede the administration of their goods to whomever they prefer in accordance with Canon 668.
6. Before taking perpetual vows the hermit will draw up a will which is also valid in civil law. (Canon 668, paragraph 1)
7. Association funds will be administered by someone appointed by the Desert Father.

VI
CONDITIONS OF MEMBERSHIP

1. Candidates are to be deeply grounded in the Catholic faith, having lived a good Christian life, exhibit strong attraction to the Bethlehem eremitical way of life and be in good physical and emotional health, preferably between the ages of 30 and 50 years.
2. The Desert Father, in harmony with the communal discernment, will decide at the present time which applicants will be admitted into pre-candidacy, provisional membership, i.e., candidacy and the novitiate, and ultimately into permanent membership.
3. Potential candidates will enter into a three month "come and see" live-in experience. Before entering the three-month live-in, the seeker will be required to participate in a program of psychological testing recommended by Bethlehem. At the end of the live-in, the pre-candidate will leave the Laura for a short period of time arrived at in consultation with the Desert Father, after which the candidate may apply to be accepted as a candidate.

4. After a period of nine to twelve months, a candidate who is not already perpetually professed may apply for admission into the novitiate and will wear the habit of the Hermits of Bethlehem. At this time, a candidate having made perpetual vows in another Institute and who has obtained an Indult of Exclaustration from that Institute, will receive the habit of the Association and will continue his/her period of probation.
5. After a novitiate of two years, which may be extended by the Desert Father for up to one year, a novice not already professed in perpetual vows, may request by letter to the Desert Father to take temporary eremitical vows of obedience, poverty and chastity for one year in the hands of the bishop and in the presence of the Desert Father in accordance with present Canon 603 and the Statutes of the Association. Temporary vows will be renewed annually up to three years before the hermit may request to take perpetual vows and enter into permanent membership in the Association.
6. After a probationary period of two years, which may be extended by the Desert Father for up to one year, a religious already in perpetual vows in another Institute may request to enter into permanent membership in the Association. An indult of departure from the former institute must be obtained prior to perpetual vows in the Association.

VII
DEPARTURE

1. Prior to admission to provisional membership candidates may leave freely.
2. Prior to admission into permanent membership, hermits in provisional membership, in consultation with the Desert Father, may leave with the permission of the bishop. Those judged to be unsuitable for the Bethlehem Way of Life by the Desert Father, in harmony with the communal discernment, may be asked to leave the Bethlehem Laura, with the approval of the bishop.
3. Permanent members may be asked to leave the Bethlehem Laura by the Desert Father, in harmony with the communal discernment, for a just cause with the approval of the council for dismissal confirmed by the diocesan bishop. The decision may be appealed to the bishop.

Rev. Eugene C. L. Romano, H.B.H.J.
Desert Father
Approved:

____

Most Reverend Frank J. Rodimer
Bishop of Paterson
Date: October 7, 1989 - Feast of Our Lady of the Rosary